Scottish Gardens

SCOTTISH GARDENS

BEING

A REPRESENTATIVE SELECTION OF DIFFERENT
TYPES, OLD AND NEW

MALLENY.

SCOTTISH GARDENS

BEING

A Representative Selection of different Types, Old and New

BY

THE RIGHT HON.

SIR HERBERT MAXWELL

BT., ., D.C.L., LL.D.

ILL BY

MARY G. W. WILSON

MEMBER OF THE PASTEL SOCIETY AND OF THE SOCIETY OF SCOTTISH ARTISTS

À vous, troupe légère,
Qui d'aile passagère
Par le monde volez,
J'offre ces violettes,
Ces lis et ces fleurettes,
Et ces roses icy—
Ces merveillettes roses—
Tout freschement écloses,
Et ces œillets aussi.—*J. du Bellay*

NEW YORK

LONGMANS, GREEN & CO.

LONDON: EDWARD ARNOLD

1908

MALLENY.

Scottish Gardens

BEING

A Representative Selection of different Types, Old and New

BY

THE RIGHT HON.

SIR HERBERT MAXWELL

BT., F.R.S., D.C.L., LL.D.

ILLUSTRATED BY

MARY G. W. WILSON

MEMBER OF THE PASTEL SOCIETY AND OF THE SOCIETY OF SCOTTISH ARTISTS

À vous, troupe légère,
Qui d'aile passagère
Par le monde volez,
J'offre ces violettes,
Ces lis et ces fleurettes,
Et ces roses icy—
Ces merveillettes roses—
Tout freschement écloses,
Et ces œillets aussi.—*J. du Bellay*

NEW YORK
LONGMANS, GREEN & CO.
LONDON: EDWARD ARNOLD
1908

SALUT

STROW mee the grounde with daffadowndillies,
And cowslips and kingcups and lovèd lillies;
    The pretty pawnce
    And the chevisaunce
Shall match with the fayre floure delice.

Shepherd's Calendar.

CONTENTS

vii

CONTENTS

APPENDIX A

APPENDIX B

APPENDIX C

LIST OF PLATES

LIST OF PLATES

SCOTTISH GARDENS

CONCERNING SCOTTISH GARDENS IN GENERAL

FTER the withdrawal of the Roman legions from Britain in the fifth century, to quote the graphic words of the late Dr. W. F. Skene, "the British Isles seemed, as it were, to retire again into the recesses of that western ocean from which they had emerged in the reign of the Emperor Claudius."[1] In the following century, Procopius, writing from Constantinople a scanty description of the lost Roman provinces of Britain, said that he believed that part of the island nearest Gaul was still inhabited and fertile, but that it was divided from the rest of the island by a wall, beyond which was a region infested by wild beasts, with an atmosphere fatal to human life, wherefore it was tenanted only by the spirits of the departed. Now the wall referred to was

---

[1] *Celtic Scotland,* i. 114.

probably that rampart erected by Lollius Urbicus for the Emperor Antoninus Pius about A.D. 140. It stretched between the Firths of Forth and Clyde, and connected the detached forts built by Julius Agricola seventy years before; but the reference may have been to the earlier wall, that great fortification drawn by the Emperor Hadrian from the Tyne to the Solway, roughly parallel with the line dividing England from Scotland at the present day.

Whichever barrier Procopius had in mind, whether it was the whole of modern Scotland, or only the Highlands, that he included in his uncomplimentary estimate of the climate, the fifteen centuries which have run their course or nearly so, since he laid down his pen have not served wholly to efface the unfavourable estimate of Scottish seasons entertained by many travelled, and all untravelled, southerners. "As in the Northerne parts of England," wrote Fynes Moryson in the seventeenth century, "they have small pleasantnes, goodnesse, or abundance of Fruites and Flowers, so in Scotland they must have lesse, or none at all."

It was Dr. Johnson, if I mistake not, and if not he, then some other equally veracious tourist, who declared that Scots farmers could only grow barley under glass; and really this assertion is not one whit further from the truth than many of the statements one may see gravely repeated in gardening journals. Advice is frequently based,

2

even in high class works on horticulture, upon the assumption that, because Scotland lies a few hundred miles nearer the North Pole than do the Home Counties, it is useless to attempt to cultivate any except the hardiest shrubs and herbs beyond the Tweed. The reader receives the impression of a rigorous climate, with intensely cold winters and sunless summers; and that impression, as regards summer, at least, is often confirmed to those who postpone their visit to Scotland till Parliament rises, perhaps late in August, after the Lammas floods have soaked the land and the evenings have turned damp and chill. But those who know the north country in June and July do not need to be warned against such an erroneous conception, or to be told that the Scottish soil and climate are quite as favourable to floral display as are those of any part of England.

Nevertheless, speaking broadly, the climates of the two realms are different in character, and it behoves the gardener to take this into account in furnishing his borders and shrubberies. It may help him to do so, if he has a general understanding of the mechanism of climate, so to speak. It certainly would have saved the present writer from many blunders had he been guided earlier by a better knowledge of the principles of meteorology, and from expense and disappointment incurred by attempting to cultivate unsuitable species of shrubs and herbs.

SCOTTISH GARDENS

The first thing to lay to heart is that Great Britain is divided, climatically, not so much into north and south, as nearly all horticultural books describe it, as into east and west. Certain plants which perish from winter cold near London and in the Midlands, flourish luxuriantly on the western sections of the counties of Inverness and Ross. This is usually explained as the direct influence of the Gulf Stream upon the seaboard climate of the British Isles. Nobody wants to speak disrespectfully of the Gulf Stream ; but hydrographers have differed among themselves in estimating the extent of its effect upon the land temperature of Western Europe, and perhaps the popular tendency has been to exaggerate it. Issuing from the Gulf of Florida, with a surface temperature of 80° F., this great current of hot water flows eastward along the banks of Newfoundland, whence it is separated by the cold and southward flowing current of Labrador. At about 40° west longitude, a well-marked branch of the Gulf Stream turns north and north-westward upon the coast of Greenland and is lost in Baffin's Bay. The main current divides again at about 25° W., 47° N., the greater moiety bending southward to form the North African current, which laves the shores of Portugal and Morocco, finally turning westward off Cape Verde and heading back to the Carribean Sea. What is left of the original stream holds a north-eastward course towards the western shores of Northern Europe, but it has parted with

4

most of its superfluous heat ; and, east of 30°
west longitude, ceases to be distinguishable from the
general eastward drift of water promoted by the
prevailing air current from w.s.w. to e.n.e.
Dr. James Croll has calculated that the Gulf
Stream is responsible for one-fifth of the total heat
of the North Atlantic, and that if the warm current
were shut off or diverted, the surface temperature
of that ocean would fall to an average of three
degrees below zero F.—that, in short, it would
become a frozen sea. Dr. Haughton, on the other
hand, has given tables showing that, while the Gulf
Stream certainly raises the temperature of our seas
very considerably in winter, it actually lowers it in
summer. Perhaps all that can be affirmed with
certainty is that the Gulf Stream has a genial
influence, not only upon the climate of the United
Kingdom, but actually within the Arctic circle at
Hammerfest.

Admitting gratefully as we may our indebtedness
to this beneficent current, it is not easy to attribute
to its sole agency the superior mildness of our western
seaboard as compared with the inland and eastern
districts. An explanation of that constant pheno-
menon must be sought not in the waters beneath
the firmament, but in the firmament itself—in the
general circulation of the atmosphere.

The air we breathe forms a fluid envelope over
the entire globe, which, becoming intensely heated
under the ecliptic, expands and rises in a huge

dome or ridge corresponding with the apparent path of the sun round the earth. From the top of this ridge the heated air flows away towards the poles, descending to the earth's surface again at about 30° N. and S. latitude. The circumference of the earth at these latitudes being very much less than at the equator, the surface velocity in diurnal rotation is necessarily diminished in proportion. But the descending air current retains, not only much of the heat, but also much of the high eastward velocity imparted to it in equatorial regions, the result being a general movement of the atmosphere in the northern temperate zone from s.w. to N.E. Land areas, being far more extensive and numerous in the northern hemisphere than they are in the southern, interfere powerfully with this general drift of atmosphere by causing local differences of temperature; but it has a clear oceanic course of about 4000 miles in passing from the coast of Florida to the Land's End. By virtue of its heat, this warm air current is able to absorb the moisture which is continually being given off by evaporation from the ocean surface, and to carry it eastward in the invisible form of vapour. But when the air current is chilled, whether in summer by meeting high land which lifts it to a colder stratum, or in winter by striking land which at that season is colder than the sea, it loses the power of carrying the vapour, which is suddenly condensed into the visible form of rain or snow, mist or fog. Such is the chief permanent cause of the greater rainfall on our western coasts, as compared with our eastern. Hence, also, their superior mildness in winter; for the latent heat, which was engaged in carrying vapour, is released as soon as that vapour is condensed and falls out of the air, being instantly felt in the form of warmth. The air current passing inland deprived of such moisture as it has lost by condensation, is deprived also of the heat which enabled it to bring that moisture to the coast; whence the far greater severity of winter at Leicester and Perth compared with western localities corresponding to these places in latitude, such as Limerick and Oban. Dr. Haughton has calculated that, on the west coast of Ireland as much heat is derived from rainfall as from the direct action of the sun.

In another important respect vegetation is affected and its character modified by the amount of vapour in the air. Moisture, in the invisible form of vapour, interferes almost as much with the passage of heat from the sun to the earth, and with the radiation of heat from the earth into space, as it does when partially condensed into the form of mist or cloud. In proportion, therefore, as the air current discharges itself of vapour by precipitation in passing over the high grounds of our western seaboard, is there less interference with the access of sunrays to the surface of midland and eastern districts. This secures for these districts brighter, hotter summers than in the west; subject always to local conditions, such as exposure to cold eastern currents. But the diminution of air-borne vapour promotes radiation, causing the earth to part more quickly with its heat, and reducing the mean winter temperature of midland and eastern districts below that of western.

Such is, very broadly and briefly, the outline of the normal course of British meteorology, as explained by Haughton, Croll, Strachey, Scott and other observers. To the horticulturist it resolves itself into this, that the climate in the west is cooler in summer and warmer in winter than that of inland and eastern districts, and he must conform to these conditions in his choice of decorative material.

It is impossible to guess how much money and labour is wasted each year in attempting to grow in a humid climate and on a cool soil plants which delight in a roasting sun on a dry formation. On the other hand, what opportunities do we not see thrown away by neglecting the capabilities of soil and climate, thereby reducing gardens and pleasure grounds to a monotonous uniformity of furniture.

Take as an example, the Rhododendron family. The common *R. ponticum* grows anywhere except on chalk or limestone; consequently it *is* grown everywhere, choking our woodlands and smothering the beautiful native undergrowth, until the eye wearies of what is in truth a very handsome shrub. Even people who live on chalk and limestone, instead of taking

8

advantage of their position to cultivate plants that revel in a cretaceous soil, are at infinite pains to prepare beds for rhododendrons, and so make their gardens as like those of other people as possible. And others, possessed of the cool soil and humid atmosphere in which rhododendrons rejoice seldom plant any but the common *ponticum* and its hybrids. All along the west coast, from the Land's End to Cape Wrath, a continual succession of bloom from midwinter to the very end of July can be secured by planting the exquisite Himalayan and Caucasian species, many of which it is vain to attempt to bring through the winter in the famous nurseries at Woking and Bagshot. Miss Wilson has caught some of these in flower in an Argyllshire garden (Stonefield, Plate IX.) and, lest the beautiful scene she has depicted should stimulate a desire in any of my west-coast readers to attempt similar effects, a list of the choicer species is given in Appendix A.

The two things requisite for success are sufficient drainage to prevent the soil getting waterlogged and shelter from violent winds, especially wind off the sea. Many species, such as *R. arboreum, campanulatum, cinnamomeum* and *cinnabarinum* will live and flower even in a windy exposure, but their foliage gets seared and stunted, and the foilage of these choice shrubs is as remarkable for beauty as their flowers.

There is a host of other exotics reputed tender in the neighbourhood of London and in the English

9

midlands, which grow and flower luxuriantly in the Scottish westland. A list of these will be found in Appendix B. How greatly the interest and beauty of pleasure-grounds might be enhanced if a selection from these were substituted for the too frequent laurel (which is not a laurel, but a plum), the ubiquitous *ponticum* rhododendron, the urban *aucuba* and the suburban *mahonia*! One would think, after surveying the sameness which pervades so many shrubberies and flower-beds that there was a poverty of material to choose from, instead of the enormous variety, almost bewildering in extent, which the enterprise of nurserymen and the diligence of their collectors have put within easy reach of people of quite moderate means.

It must be admitted that there has been a marked improvement in this respect during the last quarter of a century. Many people devote themselves nowadays to the cultivation of hardy shrubs and herbs with an enthusiasm and degree of knowledge seldom met with in early and mid-Victorian years. They have grown so keen as to fall, sometimes, into the opposite extreme, and to take more pains to rear plants with which it is difficult to succeed than they do with those best suited to their soil and climate.

I visited lately the famous garden of a friend in Sussex. I found him sitting under a tree, surrounded by borders the wealth and variety of which I was eager to explore. Before I could do so, he

marched me off saying, "Come this way ; I have
something to show you." He led me to a north-
west corner between two ivy-covered walls and
displayed with much pride a few flowering sprays
of *Tropæolum speciosum*—that lovely flame-flower,
which, in the humid north, is a rampant, but ever-
welcome weed. It certainly was a triumph of
horticulture to succeed even moderately in one of
the hottest counties in England with this plant
which revels in the cool soil and moist atmosphere
of the north ; but the merit of this garden lay
not in such feats of coddling, but in the abundance and richness of sun-loving flowers.

Do not let it be imagined that I am superior
to these little gardening foibles. *J'ai passé par là,
moi qui vous parle*—nay, I am still treading the path
of futile error. Neither age nor experience, nor
both combined, can purge a fool of his folly; and
so it comes to pass that I cannot bring myself to
root up two large specimens of *Xanthoceras sorbifolia*,
a bush which in the southern counties loads itself
in May with garlands of white flowers with a
blotch of burgundy at the base of each petal. In
Scotland I have never seen it produce more than
a meagre sprinkling of half shrivelled blossoms. So
with *Hibiscus syriacus*, that glory of English Augusts,
and the bulbous *Sternbergia*, which stars with gold
the vineyards of France, what time the cream-tinted
oxen slowly draw the oozing grapes to the wine-
press. All of these, and many others which might

be named, live in Scotland, and make abundant promise in the way of foliage ; but the promise is never, or hardly ever, fulfilled. Either the flowers lag too late for want of sun-forcing, which is the way with *Hibiscus*, or the plants are never ripened enough to form flower-buds at all, which is the matter with *Sternbergia*. On the other hand, there are many plants which relish the cool, moist north, and refuse to respond to the sun of southerly shires.

The vaporous western and northern atmosphere, acting in conjunction with a soil for the most part cool, has one effect upon plant growth note-worthy for Scottish gardeners, greatly modifying the cultural requirements of certain plants. General instructions contained in horticultural works and nursery catalogues are mostly calculated for the meridian of London, and directions for providing shade apply chiefly to the sunnier regions of our realm and hot soils. But a plant that appreciates a northern exposure or overhanging foliage in Sussex may require all the direct sunshine it can receive in Argyllshire or Perthshire to ripen its growth sufficiently for the supreme effort of flowering. For instance, when I first obtained the beautiful Chilian shrub then called *Crinodendron Hookeri*, but now known as *Tricuspidaria lanceolata*, I was advised by that veteran horticulturist, Canon Ellacombe, to give it a north exposure. Accordingly I planted one against a wall facing north-east, and it has grown at the rate of two feet a year—a picture of vigour—but with very sparse return in flowers. Another plant of the same species, set in an open border facing south-west, has not grown nearly so fast, but is of sturdier habit, and at the present moment (22nd August) is closely set with tiny flower-buds on long white peduncles, which will swell next April into the crimson globular bells which are the glory of this choice evergreen.[1] Canon Ellacombe's advice was perfectly sound and applicable to the neighbourhood of Bath, but had to be applied with a *caveat* in grey Galloway.

Again, *Daphne Blaageana* seeks all the shade it can get in its native haunts in south-eastern Europe, and may demand the same when grown on dry, chalky soils in southern England; but I have never seen it so fine as under Mr. Moore's care in the Glasnevin Botanic Gardens, where it covers a large round bed, in full sunshine, with its delectable ivory-white blossoms.

Similar examples might be multiplied; the lesson of them all being the same, namely, that the vaporous atmosphere of Scotland, especially in the west, tempers the sun-rays enough to enable most shade-loving plants not only to endure them, but to benefit by them.

A wise discrimination in deciding what to grow makes all the difference between struggling and co-operating with nature. For what, after all,

[1] This never came to pass. The destructive frost of Eastertide, 1908, destroyed the flower-buds of this and many another choice shrub.

does cultivation amount to? I speak not of the
florist's craft, which takes a wild flower or shrub
and, with infinite cunning, transforms it into something different, so that a wild mother carnation
could not recognise her own offspring in the mon-
strous Malmaison race (unless it were by scent, as a
ewe does her lamb), nor the modest little wild
heartsease, which covers with a blue mist the roofs
of old log-houses in Norway, claim kinship with the
show and fancy pansies which have developed such
amazing colours and are judged, like poultry, by
their points. For the gardener proper all this work
is done by others; his function is to propagate and
grow; his care is so to dispose plants that they shall
be spared the intense struggle for life which every
wild tree, shrub or herb has to undergo. It is
surprising what fine qualities many of our British
wild flowers develop under careful handling. We
cause the ends of the earth to be ransacked for the
furnishing of our borders, while all around us, in
meadow and copse, on seacoast and moorland, by
riverside and hedgerow, there is material which will
respond to thoughtful treatment with a display
rivalling that of costly exotics. Among the many
excellent, but unfulfilled, intentions of a desultory
life has been the purpose to create an all-British
garden, wherein nothing should be planted but native
vegetation. Any amateur who may feel disposed
for the experiment will find some suggestion in
Appendix C. Meanwhile, let me give a single illus-

tration of possibilities. In the peat bogs of lowland Scotland, northern England and Ireland may be found a slender, little, heathlike plant, four or five inches high, sparsely clad with narrow, evergreen leaves, glaucous on the back, bearing in late summer a few pretty, pale pink, drooping flowers on the model of an arbutus or a bearberry. Strange to say, this plant is not found in the Highlands of Scotland, though it is abundant in Norway. It is the marsh andromeda (*A. polifolia*), according to modern classification the solitary species in the genus. It seems to prefer the sloppiest parts of the bog, where even heather declines to grow; but in fact it grows there only because there is no room for it elsewhere. Its hardy constitution enables it to maintain a precarious existence in a soaked mixture of sour peat and sphagnum which would be the death of any other hardwooded plant. Nevertheless, it is as fond of good things as its neighbours. Remove some plants from their native slime (they are so feeble that it must be carefully done) and set them in a sunny border in a mixture of peat, sand and loam, keep them from being overshadowed by grosser plants, lay some stones on the surface round them to keep some moisture about their roots, and in a couple of years they will grow into sturdy little bushes, nearly a foot high, with abundant leafage and a fine display of flowers. You have aided them in the struggle for life, and they reward you by developing into plants of really extraordinary beauty.

SCOTTISH GARDENS

In visiting Scottish gardens (and the same remark applies to English ones also) I have been struck by the almost universal mismanagement, sometimes the total neglect, of flowering shrubs. The majority of gardeners seem to act on the principle that these plants must take care of themselves. A shrubbery is laid out, planted with a variety of species, and left severely alone. What is the consequence? The strong growers throttle the more slender ones, which either disappear, or lead a precarious existence, spindling away among their rampant neighbours with little opportunity of ripening wood to carry flowers.

Again, many of the rarer shrubs, especially rhododendrons, are grafted upon common vigorous stocks. Constant vigilance is required, but is very seldom bestowed, to prevent suckers springing from the stock and supplanting the more delicate scion. It is a treat to spend a morning in a shrubbery like that at Poltalloch, in Argyllshire, where the gardener, Mr. Melville, tends the shrubs as carefully as the ordinary man does his roses and fruit trees, giving each plant plenty of room to develop and securing that by judicious pruning and timely transplanting. The result is, to mention one species only, that he can show you bushes of the rare *Eucryphia pinnatifolia* twelve or fourteen feet high, covered with charming white blossoms on their entire height and circumference. Many people, no doubt, have planted *Eucryphia*, allowed it to

16

disappear and concluded that it was unable to endure a northern climate; but the fact is that, like so many other Chilian plants, both *Eucryphia pinnatifolia* and the rarer *cordifolia* take most kindly to cultivation in Scotland and Ireland, though they cannot be kept at Kew.

In another respect carelessness is even more apparent in the generality of shrubberies. Few gardeners seem to be aware that, in the cultivation of flowering shrubs, there is any need for the pruning knife or *sécateur*, except to keep a gangway on garden paths. But many flowering shrubs need pruning as regularly as roses if they are to do themselves justice. Especially is this the case with those that bloom on the season's growth. These should be carefully gone over immediately after they have flowered, cut back to an eye behind the old flowering shoots and relieved of weakly and crowded growths. Typical examples of shrubs requiring this treatment are *Buddleia, Forsythia,* the choicer kinds of *Philadelphus, Escallonia phillipiana,* the hybrid *Deutzias,* and all the *Olearias.* Shrubs which flower on two-year-old growth require all weakly or failing growth removed and vigorous growth pinched or shortened.

Of course there are many species of flowering trees and shrubs which, planted in quantity and growing to a large size, cannot be gone over regularly; but anything choice or rare will amply repay a little intelligent handling. The finer sorts of rhododen-

B   17

drons, especially, suffer frequently from being planted six feet or so apart when small and allowed to grow up in a jungle. This class of evergreen does not benefit by pruning, but none bears transplanting so well or so easily. As the foliage of many kinds of rhododendron is exceedingly beautiful, each plant should have ample room from first to last. Various kinds of lilies, most of which thrive best in soil full of living roots, may be employed to fill the spaces which it is desirable to keep between rhododendrons when planted in a bed.

In mild districts the hardy palm, *Chamærops excelsa, Cordyline*, and the finer bamboos may be used with splendid effect. Tree ferns, also grow luxuriantly with side shelter from high winds and overhead shelter from frost. Both of these requisites are easily provided because these cryptogams thrive best in shade and therefore should be planted in a moist wood. Not many years ago, tree ferns were easily obtained in London sale-rooms; but they are hard to come by now, in consequence of the wise action of the New Zealand government in prohibiting the exportation of *Dicksonia*. Nurserymen who have old plants ask a guinea a foot for them, but some tradesmen have seedlings to dispose of. These can be had at a reasonable rate; should be grown forward in a cold frame or cool greenhouse, hardened off at a foot high, when they may be planted out in permanent positions.

As no flower garden depends only on flowers

for its charm, so is it of the utmost moment that suitable kinds of trees should be chosen to decorate it. Assuming that the environment of the garden proper is more or less woodland in character,[1] the gardener's concern will be to choose from the vast variety offered by modern nurserymen. In spacious grounds, room will not be grudged to an ancient oak or two, or a group of beeches or limes. But in a garden of modest dimensions the presence of these and other trees with far-reaching, hungry roots will impoverish the borders and cause the loss of many a precious thing. Luckily we have among the many coniferous trees introduced to this country during last century some which content themselves with a very moderate root-run. The columnar habit of such evergreens as the Lawson cypress, the incense cypress (*Libocedrus decurrens*) and the pencil cedar (*Juniperus virginianus*) are of priceless effect among flowerbeds, providing those vertical lines which, as given by the Italian cypress, impart such a charming character to Mediterranean scenery. But it is sad to see how this effect has been marred or missed owing to the pernicious practice of growing such conifers as these from cuttings. Young plants, trim and verdant, come

---

[1] Although this is very desirable for providing shelter it is not indispensable for fine effect. In the very heart of the treeless waste surrounding Kinbrace railway station in Sutherland, stands the shooting lodge of Badanloch. Never have I seen greater profusion of brilliant perennials than surprised me when I visited this place during the wet and cheerless summer of 1907. The garden was on a slope, open to all the winds of heaven, the soil being chiefly grit and peat.

from the nursery and perhaps do not betray their true character for several years. Gradually they assume the appearance of branches stuck in the ground, which indeed they are, or they send up a crowd of sticks instead of one straight leader. The only way to avoid disappointment in this matter is either to grow one's own seedlings, whereby five or six years delay is incurred, or to employ a trustworthy tradesman and insist on being supplied with plants grown from seed.

Another delightful tree, which used to be classed as a conifer, but has now been ascertained to be nearly related to the cycads and palms, is the gingko or maidenhair tree. It is deciduous : it is often misshapen, because grown from a cutting : but for grace and distinction a well-grown specimen is hard to beat, and it is perfectly hardy in many parts of Scotland.

Conifers, however valuable for winter greenery, afford unsatisfactory shade ; and a shady place or places there must be in every garden however small. This can only be had in perfection from broad-leaved trees, and there is abundant variety to choose from. In a woodland country it is perhaps desirable to mark the select character of garden ground by giving a preference to exotic growths. Where beech and oak, elm and sycamore, form the background of garden scenery, it is an agreeable change to see fine specimens of sweet and horse-chestnut, robinia, tulip-tree, gleditsia, and the finer maples. The red flowering horse-chestnut, *Æsculus carnea*, a hybrid between the common horse-chestnut and the American *Æsculus pavia*, is far too seldom seen in Scottish pleasure grounds, though commonly planted in the neighbourhood of London. It is, however, perfectly at home in the north, and although it is generally considered to be of less lofty growth than the common sort, my experience with it leads me to believe that there is not much difference between the two kinds in that respect. If there is no more splendid spectacle in British woodland scenery than a well-grown horse-chestnut in full bloom, the red-flowered variety is no whit inferior, and the beauty of each is mutually enhanced by contrast.

One word about another tree too seldom seen, matchless as it is in certain qualities of foliage and outline—to wit—the evergreen oak. Its effect in a garden is well shown in Miss Wilson's view at Castle Kennedy (Plate X.). Changeless in its kindly neutral tint, save when the wind tosses the boughs to make them show the silvery undersides of the leaves, or for a brief period in early summer when the flowers and young growth spread a tawny tint over the grey, the holm oak never fails to attract admiration when it is well-grown. But it is not always grown to its best. Planted singly or at wide intervals, it is apt to assume the form of a huge bush ; but submit it to the early discipline of close planting—a dozen or so in a group six feet apart—and you may get a magnificent tree like the one at Rosanna, co. Wicklow, which is 90 feet high, loftier than any of the species in its native Southern Europe, so freely does it respond to the genial influences of the west.

The task of making a selection of garden scenes in Scotland has been one of much perplexity. In order to make it representative of all styles and scales, many famous and beautiful places have been passed by. Moreover, the summer of 1907 was the wettest and coldest we have had for thirty years; which frustrated many attempts to portray gardens in the remoter parts of the country. Had it been Miss Wilson's lot to have executed her task during the summer of 1908, not only would the work have been more agreeable but it would have had more satisfactory results. The purpose of artist and author has been to present specimens of gardens of every degree—modest as well as majestic, formal as well as free—whereby the possessor of the humblest plot of ground may be stimulated to beautify it with as fair hope of proportionate success as the lord of thousands of acres.

ARDGOWAN

RENFREWSHIRE

LTHOUGH botanists cannot be got to recognise the snowdrop as a true native of Britain, no foreigner establishes itself more cordially wherever in our land it finds the combination of a moist, cool atmosphere with a free soil. Those persons who have never happened to visit the west coast of Scotland during January and February can have little idea of the profuse display made by this little bulb wherever it is given a chance, or of the rapidity with which it takes possession of the floor of a hollow wood. Probably the conditions are equally favourable and produce a similar result in Ireland and along the Welsh coast, but of this I cannot speak with assurance, never having visited those districts during the snowdrop season. Anyhow, you must not look for snowdrops in sun-baked latitudes. Some years ago, narcissus and other flowers arrived in the market from Scilly unusually early. Now the snowdrop is perhaps the only spring-flowering bulb which cannot be coaxed or forced into blossom a day earlier

23

than its natural date. If the ground happens to be iron-bound with frost in January, then the snowdrops potted and kept under glass will get a start of their brethren in the open air; but not before the time when the latter would have flowered had it been physically possible for them to get through the hard surface-soil. Probably this is the only, it is certainly the chief, impediment to the snowdrop's punctuality, causing a considerable variation in the date of flowering. On the west coast of Scotland I have gathered the first snowdrop on 19th December in one winter; in other seasons not until 8th or 10th January.

In the year aforesaid, I asked Mr. Dorrien Smith, than whom nobody has a more thorough understanding of bulbs and their behaviour, whether he had noticed in Scilly any precocity in the snowdrop bloom corresponding to that of the narcissus.

"Snowdrops!" said he, "we can't grow them in Scilly. We are too hot for them."

Neither do they prosper on most parts of the east coast; they will grow, indeed, and flower, but they do not multiply or luxuriate. No: if you want to enjoy snowdrops at their finest, you must go, not where there is most snow, as in the midland and eastern regions, nor where there is least snow, in Scilly and southern England, but to the west where clouds in winter droop low and weep long, where the tooth of frost seldom strikes so deep as to arrest all growth.

ARDGOWAN.

than its natural date. If the ground happens to
be permeated with frost in January, then the snowdrops potted and kept under glass will get a start
of their brethren in the open air; but not before
the time when the latter would have flowered had
it been physically possible for them to get through
the hard surface soil. If not only this is the only, it
is certainly the chief cause to the snowdrop's
punctuality, causing a considerable variation in the
date of flowering. On the west coast of Scotland
I have gathered the first snowdrop on 19th December
in one winter; in other seasons not until 8th or 10th
January.

In the year afore said I asked Mr. Dorrien Smith,
than whom nobody has a more thorough understanding of bulbs and their behaviour, whether he had
noticed the precocity in the snowdrop bloom
ere he had noticed that of the narcissus.

"said he, "we can't grow them in
too hot for them."

they prosper on most parts of the
they will grow, indeed, and flower, but
or luxuriate. No: if you want
enjoy snowdrops at their finest, you must go, not
where there is most snow, as in the midland and
eastern regions, nor where there is least snow, in
Scilly and southern England, but to the west where
clouds in winter droop low and weep long, where
the bite of frost seldom strikes so deep as to arrest
the growth.

ARDGOWAN.

ARDGOWAN

Snowdrops possess one virtue which is appreciated by all who take note of flowering herbs; the accursed rabbit, which is responsible for incalculable destruction and for the extirpation of much of our native flora, cannot digest them. What the repellent property is nobody seems to know. The Amaryllis family, whereof the snowdrop is a member, differs only from the Iris family in having six stamens instead of three; yet rabbits will devour every shred of crocus, sparaxis and sisyrinchium — iridaceous bulbs—while they leave snowdrops and daffodils, true amaryllids, severely alone. In daffodils the protective agent is known to consist, not of any chemical poison, but of numerous minute crystals of lime, called *raphides,* contained in the sap, which prove so powerful an irritant as to upset even the digestion of a rabbit. Whatever be the corresponding provision in the snowdrop's slender growth it is one for which all lovers of the country must feel grateful, for it has been the means of preserving the chief ornament of our woodlands when the days are at their darkest.

Nowhere may you realise this more fully than at Ardgowan, the Renfrewshire home of Sir Hugh and Lady Alice Shaw Stewart. Nowhere else shall you find snowdrops more abundant or more charmingly disposed — millions of them — among sloping woods on the shore of the Firth of Clyde.

The garden proper at Ardgowan is notable in many respects, and bids fair to become still more so under the guidance of its mistress, who has applied herself with ardour and intelligence to develop the resources of a kindly soil and genial climate. The walled garden is 200 yards from end to end, with great ranges of glass, where Mr. Lunt, who has been in active superintendence for more than half a century, produces fruit by the hundred-weight, unsurpassed in quality. Round the outside of this enclosure lies an outer garden, where many choice shrubs have been allowed to maintain for many years a fierce struggle for existence. These are now in process of being relieved and rearranged, during which many unsuspected treasures have been brought to light, such as a bush of *Rhododendron glaucum* (distinguished among others of the genus by its deliciously scented foliage) of the unusual height of eight feet.

The mansion house stands on a plateau sixty feet above the main garden, commanding enchanting views across the blue firth of the Argyllshire hills to the west, and many-crested Arran to the south. The lawn garden stretches before the south front of the house, where two enormous arbutus, of well-nigh forest stature, attest the mildness of the climate. There is also a fair specimen of the deciduous or swamp cypress, a tree seldom seen in Scotland.

It would take a long summer day to exhaust the beauty and interest of these grounds; but the same may be said of many another earthly paradise which have grown up round old country houses.

26

ARDGOWAN

Miss Wilson might have hesitated long before deciding on a single subject where there is so much to choose from; she has chosen rightly, I think, to depict a scene and a season in which Ardgowan has no rival known to me; for nowhere else have I been able to walk a mile on end through acres of snowdrops in blossom.

Round three sides of the plateau referred to runs a steep slope, in places precipitous, of red conglomerate. At the apex of this green promontory, where the cliff is sheer, is poised the ancient keep of Inverkip. At the neck of the promontory stands the Georgian mansion of Ardgowan, built in 1798, a period when Scottish lairds were beginning to find the fortalices of their ancestors inconveniently cramped for modern households. Between the cliff and the sea is a wide belt of that raised beach which forms such a marked feature in coast scenery of the west, known to geologists as the 25 foot beach, formed when the general land level was that distance below the present one. Woods of pine and broad leaved trees clothe the flat land, the slopes and the cliff itself, wherever foothold can be found, and all these woods are carpeted with snowdrops, primroses, and blue hyacinths. Empty enough they seem in winter time. Cover-shooters, pursuing their pastime in the dark days of November, little think what wealth of flowers is stored in millions of modest little bulbs beneath their feet; but he must indeed be insensible to natural beauty who,

27

returning in February, is not moved to enthusiasm by the display.

Flowers have appealed to human admiration and affection in all ages; the exhortation to "consider the lilies" was not addressed to unsympathetic understandings; but in other respects our æsthetic standard varies strangely from generation to generation. A curious illustration of this is given in an anecdote of Lancelot Brown, the architect and landscape gardener, commonly known as "Capability Brown."[1] It is said that Sir John Shaw Stewart, when he was planning his new house, employed Brown to lay out the park and plantations. A conspicuous and charming feature in the view to the north from the front door of the house is a steep, wooded hill called Idzholm, at the foot of which flows the little river Kip, much frequented by sea-trout. The silvan curtain over Idzholm is broken near the centre by a great grey crag, contrasting delightfully with the soft park scenery and surrounding cultivation. But that is not how Capability Brown viewed it. Unable to plant over the bare rock, he proposed to paint it green, so that, when viewed from a distance, it might present the appearance of a woodland glade! Inconceivable, you will say, but in justice to Mr. Brown let it not be forgotten how greatly

---

[1] "Capability Brown" died in 1783; the present mansion of Ardgowan was not begun till 1798, so the story perhaps had its origin in another designer. Brown, however, may have laid out the park before the new house was begun.

the country has altered since his day. That was an age when an English traveller returning to London from a tour in Scotland, described his impressions thus succinctly:

"Bleak mountains and desolate rocks
Were the wretched result of our pains;
The swains greater brutes than their flocks,
The nymphs as polite as their swains."

At the close of the eighteenth century, the greater part of Renfrewshire was brown moorland. Grey rocks were too common to be thought picturesque; the landscape gardener's business was to make his employer's park appear like a smooth oasis in the surrounding wilderness. In these our days, when every farmer's ambition is to make two blades of grass, or two turnips, grow where one grew before, we have changed our feeling in this matter. We pile up mimic crags and miniature alps in feeble imitation of the boulders and heather which our ancestors were at so much pains to get rid off, and pronounce that part of our pleasure grounds most delectable which most nearly resembles the primæval wild. Rockeries, water-gardens, wild-gardens, bog-gardens—all are symptoms of reaction from excessive trimness and formality.

Upon the new house was bestowed the name of Ardgowan, as the lands were called which Robert III. bestowed in 1403 upon his natural son Sir John Stewart, having previously given him the estates of Auchingoun and Blackhall in 1390 and

1395 respectively. All these lands have passed in male succession through six centuries to the present owner, but for five hundred years the knights of Ardgowan were content to live in the old tower of Inverkip, which is shown in Miss Wilson's drawing. It has been the scene of many a fierce conflict, being first mentioned in history in 1307 as the refuge of Sir Philip de Mowbray, one of Edward I.'s best captains, who, in May 1307, fell into an ambush, laid near Kilmarnock, by Good Sir James of Douglas. Barbour tells the story with much relish—how one of Douglas's men caught hold of Mowbray's scabbard, and must have captured him had not the belt broken, and so the English knight rode free.

> Tharfor furth the wais tuk he then
> To Kilmarnok and Kilwynnyn,
> And till Ardrossan eftir syn [afterwards].
> Syn [then] throu the Largis him alane
> Till Ennirkyp the way has tane.[1]

The castle was "stuffit all with Inglismen"—that is, it held an English garrison, who received the fugitive "in gret dante."

But if one yields to the temptation to dive into the annals of an old Scottish house, he will be led far astray from the matter of this volume, which is, or ought to be, horticulture.

[1] Barbour's *Brus*, lx. 94-98.

WHITEHOUSE

MIDLOTHIAN

HE modest demesne of Whitehouse abuts upon the high road which, for the best part of a mile, flanks the old royal chace of Cramond Regis, now a country gentleman's spacious park, whereof the name has been altered by an unpoetical generation into Barnton.

Whitehouse belonged of old to the Knights Templars. On the suppression of the Order in the fourteenth century, the lands were bestowed upon William Earl of Douglas, who, in turn, granted them to James Sandilands, husband of his sister Alianora, a lady who must be credited with extraordinary attraction, physical or other, seeing that she married five husbands in succession. From James Sandilands is descended the present Lord Torphichen, twelfth baron in the creation of 1564, who retains the superiority of Whitehouse, the *reddendo*, or annual feu-duty, being a white rose. After passing through several hands, the property was purchased by Mr. Mackay, the present owner, who has renovated and enlarged the seventeenth century mansion with tasteful discretion.

The chief features of the garden of Whitehouse are at their best, like daffodils, "before the swallow dares." Nowhere else in Scotland, and only in one place in England (Stocken Hall, Lincolnshire) have I seen such wealth of winter aconite. A belt of trees round the garden is thickly carpeted with them; they run through the ivy and grass, which sparkle with myriads of their little golden cups and dainty green frills; only the surrounding stone walls and hard gravel paths suffice to keep them within limits.

It was a day of sullen gusts and bitter snow showers when I visited Whitehouse; the lawn of crocuses, which Miss Wilson has depicted so charmingly, was but a mass of tightly closed purple cones, for the crocus is too careful of its golden anthers and stigma to open except in full sunshine. To the crocus, as to most herbs which hold their blooms erect, is given the power of shutting out foul weather; but the winter aconite heeds neither cold nor storm. Appearing above ground when the days are not long past their shortest, it seems determined to enjoy every ray of light that it can gather, before it obeys the law of its being, and goes to its long sleep underground throughout the summer and autumn months. Certainly that innumerable company of golden blossoms remains the one bright memory of that unkindly February day.

WHITEHOUSE

It is a flower whereof enough use is not made by country lovers. Perhaps we despise it for being so cheap; you can get a thousand of its gnarled tubers for a few shillings. But these require a little care in starting. Many people have been disappointed at the result of planting out tubers in a dry state as they come from a tradesman. They simply rot if they are set out in close turf. The proper way to naturalise them is to grow them for a season in rows in rather a sandy border; in the following spring, when the bloom is fading, take them up carefully with as much soil as will stick to them, and plant them where you would have them grow permanently. No place is more favourable than a hollow wood of deciduous trees, where the turf is not too dense. Here they will rapidly increase by seed and offsets; rabbits will not touch them, and the display will be something to look forward to in the darkest time of the year. A newly introduced species, *Eranthis cilicica*, has been described as better than our old friend *hyemalis*. I cannot see wherein is its superiority; the frill, instead of being bright grass green, has a bronze tint, undesirable at a season when verdure is particularly to be coveted, and as yet the plant is ten times the price of the other.

Unlike the aconite, it is only in enclosed grounds like those of Whitehouse, where the accursed rabbit comes not, that the crocus can obtain and maintain a footing. Even so, the bulbs are often the prey of mice and voles; but where these charming flowers

D

can hold their own, they increase rapidly and provide a feast of colour every spring. A feast to which, as I was grieved to notice a few days ago, some people show strange indifference. On the outskirts of a small country town in south-western Scotland stands an old grey house, surrounded by about an acre of garden and pleasure-ground, upon which until twenty years ago, the owner used to expend much care, planting therein many a choice shrub and herb. He died; the property passed into other hands and the garden into neglect. But the purple crocuses have taken possession of the whole turf, and, as I passed that way one bright March morning all the enclosure was steeped in Tyrian dye. All of it, except where a goat was tethered on the lawn; which beast had browsed everything bare within the radius of its rope! Surely, methought, the human retina is alike in all ranks and conditions of men, except the colour-blind. Is there not one member of this household who cares to prevent the marring of this exquisite display?

Matters are very different at Whitehouse, where the crocuses have taken possession of every available breadth of turf and are the pride and delight of the family. Miss Wilson has chosen for her subject the spot where these pretty flowers cluster thickly round an old sun-dial, which bears the inscription, MR. DAVID STRACHAN, 1732, the name of a former owner of Whitehouse. It might now be inscribed with a legend applicable alike to the dial and the sun-

WHITEHOUSE

WHITEHOUSE.

—

loving flowers—*Horas non numero nisi serenas*—" I take no account of hours that are not sunny."

Like the dial, these crocuses are no affair of yesterday. Who shall declare how many generations of men have passed away since the original bulbs were planted. Brought thither they must have been by hand, for, although the purple *Crocus vernus* is admitted to the list of British plants, it is not native to North Britain. Spring after spring, for an untold number of years, they have multiplied and spread, covering the turf with their imperial flush. It may be that King James V. in his incognito wanderings may have noted the pretty flowers as he passed that way. For he had a pretty adventure just outside this garden.

He was a monarch of many fancies, some of which were highly offensive to Angus "Bell-the-Cat," and other haughty lords. Among these fancies, it was James's humour to wander about the country disguised as a peasant, or, at best, a bonnet laird. Thus, coming one day alone to the bridge of Cramond, he was beset by a party of gypsies, who were for relieving him of the contents of his pockets. All men went armed in those days, as constantly as do Albanians and Montenegrins at the present; so the King out with his sword, and running upon the steep and narrow bridge, managed to make good his defence for a while. Yet numbers must have prevailed in the end; and it was well for King James that a real husbandman, threshing corn in a barn hard by, heard the cries for succour uttered by the counterfeit. This man hurried up, flail in hand, and plied it to such good effect that the robbers decamped. Then the peasant took the King, in whom he beheld but one of his own class, into his house, brought him water and a towel to wash away traces of the fray, and escorted him part of the way back to Edinburgh. As they walked, the King asked for the name of his deliverer.

"John Howieson is my name," was the reply, "and I am just a bondsman on the farm o' Braehead, whilk belongs to the King o' Scots himsel'."

"Is there anything in the world you would wish more than another for yourself?" asked the King.

"'Deed, if I was laird o' the bit land I labour as a bondsman I'd be the blythest man in braid Scotland. But what will *your* name and calling be, neebour?" enquired the peasant in his turn.

"Oh," replied the King, "I'm weel kent about the Palace o' Holyrood as the Gudeman o' Ballengeich. I hae a small appointment in the palace, ye ken; and if ye hae a mind to see within, I'll be proud to show ye round on Sabbath nixtocum, and maybe ye'll get a bit guerdon for the gude service ye hae dune me this day."

"Faith! I'd like that fine," said John, and on the following Sunday presented himself at the palace gate to enquire for the Gudeman o' Ballengeich. The King had arranged for his admission, and received him dressed in the same rustic disguise as before. Having shown John Howieson round the palace, he asked him whether he would like to see the King. "Aye, that wad I," exclaimed John, "if nae offence be gi'en or ta'en. But hoo' will I ken his grace[1] amang the nobeelity?"

"Oh, you'll ken him fine, John," replied the King, "for he'll be the only man covered amang them a'."

Then the King brought his guest to the great hall where were assembled many peers and officers of state, bravely attired in silk and velvet of many hues, passmented with gold and silver lace. John had on the best clothes he had, but felt abashed amid so great splendour, and tried in vain to distinguish the King.

"Wasna I having ye telt that ye wad ken his grace by his going covered," said James.

John took another look round the hall; then turned to his guide, saying:

"God, man! it maun either be you or me that's King o' Scots, for there's nane ither here carryin' his bonnet."

Then the secret came out, followed by the promised guerdon, which was no less than a grant to John Howieson and his descendants of the farm of Braehead, to be held of the Crown for ever, on

---

[1] The title of "Majesty" was first assumed in England by Henry VIII., and in Scotland was first applied to the monarch in Queen Mary's reign. Some may be disposed to regret the change, holding that grace is a more kingly attribute than majesty.

condition that the owner should ever be ready to present a basin and ewer for the King to wash his hands withal, either at Holyrood house or when crossing the brig o' Cramond.

"Accordingly," says Sir Walter Scott in the *Tales of a Grandfather*, "in the year 1822, when George IV. came to Scotland, the descendant of John Howieson of Braehead, who still possesses the estate which was given to his ancestor, appeared at a solemn festival, and offered his Majesty water from a silver ewer, that he might perform the service by which he held his lands."

Less seemly, but not less characteristic of the social system of the sixteenth century, is another memory connected with this place. The fourth Earl of Huntly, the great champion of the Roman Church in Scotland, had a brother, Alexander Gordon, who was Bishop-designate of Caithness from 1544 to 1548; elected Archbishop of Glasgow in 1550, his title was disputed and he resigned the see to the Pope in 1551. He was then created Archbishop of Athens, a sinecure, and became Bishop of the Isles in 1553, which see he held till 1562 together with that of Galloway, whereof he acquired the temporalities in 1559. He also held the abbacies of Tongland, Inchaffray and Icolmkill—whence it may be inferred that he was a peculiarly affluent prelate. He also showed sagacity in noting the signs of the times, for he turned Protestant, being the only consecrated bishop who joined the Lords of the Congregation at the Reformation.

WHITEHOUSE

"But what," exclaims the perplexed reader, "has all this to do with the crocuses at Whitehouse?" Only this, that the crocuses set a desultory mind astray among the memories of Cramond, and, at the time when this astute pluralist was attending the Court of Holyrood, there lived one David Logie at King's Cramond. With David lived a fair daughter Barbara, whom Bishop Gordon made his mistress, and had by her four sons, three of whom he succeeded in getting made bishops. But in one thing he did not succeed, though he tried hard. He never could get Barbara recognised as his wife, even after his change of religion released him technically from his vow of celibacy.

MONREITH

NE writing about daffodils should foreswear poetic quotation, were it only in common consideration for his readers. Nevertheless there is one practical point connected with this favourite flower rendering excusable a reference to a passage in the greatest of English poets. When Shakespeare wrote of daffodils

> That come before the swallow dares, and take
> The winds of March with beauty,

he had in mind, not the March of our calendar, but March old style, which, according to Julian reckoning, was in the seventeenth century, ten days in retard of the Gregorian dates. Although the Scottish Privy Council decreed the adoption of the new style from 1600, it was not until 1751 that the British Parliament followed suit, passing an Act in that year which set matters in order by the omission of all dates between the 2nd and the 14th of September, 1752. Thus when *The Winter's Tale* was produced in 1611, Shakespeare's month of March corresponded to the period

40

MONREITH.

... about daffodils should fore-
... poetic quotation, were it only in
... common consideration for his readers.
Nevertheless there is one practical point
connected with this favourite flower
... excusable a reference to a passage in the
... English poets. When Shakespeare wrote

... come before the swallow dares, and take
... winds of March with beauty,

... March of our calendar, but
... according to Julian reckoning,
... century, ten days in retard of
the ... Although the Scottish Privy
Council ... the adoption of the new style from
1600, ... until 1751 that the British Parliament
foll... passing an Act in that year which set
... in order by the omission of all dates between
... and the 14th of September, 1752. Thus
... The *Winter's Tale* was produced in 1611, Shake-
...are's month of March corresponded to the period

40

MONREITH.

now noted by us as extending from 11th March to 10th April, both inclusive. This puts the poet's chronology in harmony with our present experience : for the common daffodil is never at its prime till the beginning of April, even in early districts. In backward districts the full flush is not to be expected before the middle of the month. It was on the 2nd April that Miss Wilson made her study of daffodils at Monreith, and they would have made a braver show had she been able to wait till the following week.

There is no plant, not even the rose, which has undergone more frequent transformation at the hands of the hybridiser than the daffodil ; but the natural species were perfect before man took to playing pranks with them, and I confess to thinking the new varieties no improvement on the old types. Those which have run riot through the Monreith woods are the common sort, *Narcissus pseudo-narcissus*, which is probably a native of England, and certainly revels in the humid climate of Scotland. One wants nothing better ; yet there are some varieties of this species which it would be folly to reject. The one known as *bicolor*, for instance, with a golden tube and broad, ivory-white segments, is quite as beautiful and as easily naturalised as the type, but it flowers a fortnight or three weeks later. Then there are the miniature forms, *minor*, *nanus*, and *minimus*, with tube and segments alike of rich golden yellow. These should be grown in borders, with such contemporary

E

flowers as hepaticas, chionodoxa, early squills and dog-tooth violets. As for the double varieties, out upon them! To quote Perdita once more—

> I'll not put
> The dibble in earth to set one slip of them.

The sculptured design of this flower is so admirable that it is sheer sin to let it be disfigured by doubling.

Talking of daffodils, one cannot but breathe a thanksgiving to Nature for that she has furnished them with an infallible protection against the well-nigh omnivorous rabbit. One would suppose that the succulent green blades, pushing up through winter-slain herbage, were just the diet to whet the unholy appetite of these brutes. But they know better than to set a tooth to them. As the protective agent in certain plants is very obscure, perhaps I may be allowed to quote here what I have said elsewhere on this matter.

"In regard to daffodils, they appear to be protected, not by any chemical poison, but by a purely mechanical agency which has been brought to light by the researches of the Rev. W. Wilks, editor of the Royal Horticultural Society's *Journal.* In February, 1905, he heard from a nurseryman, who grows daffodils for the flower trade, that men and boys employed to gather the flowers suffered from poisoned hands. He explained that after the men had been at work a little while, their hands became sore, gatherings forming under the finger-nails and wherever the skin was broken or chapped. This statement having been confirmed by another daffodil-grower, one of the largest in the trade, Mr. Wilks instituted research into the cause, and came to the conclusion that the irritant in the sap of the daffodil is not a true poison at all, but that the mischief is caused by small crystals of lime, called *raphides*, of which the sap is full. He recommends that people employed to gather daffodils should oil their hands before setting to work, and rub tallow under their finger-nails."

Monreith has been in possession of the same family for 427 years. That it has been for a considerable part of that period a home of flowers, there is the evidence of a fine piece of tapestry to prove. This was the work of the wife of the third baronet (he died in 1771), who set herself to depict in *appliqué* the flowers growing in the castle garden. They were laid on a maroon ground to serve as a carpet—literally a *parterre*—for the castle drawing-room. A laborious task, but evidently a labour of love, so faithfully are the dame's favourites set out in a design of remarkable grandeur. A large basket of flowers forms the centre ; smaller groups fill the four corners, and round the carpet runs a continuous wreath looped with ribbons.

Stowed away in a lumber room, this fine piece of work was unearthed thirty years ago. Moths had played havoc with the ground cloth, but the needlework was almost intact, and the colours fresh : skilful hands were set busy relaying the flowers upon cloth of an old gold colour, and the piece now hangs on the wall of the ante-room in the modern house of Monreith. Among the flowers most easily recognised in the design are the madonna lily (which refuses to flourish with us now), the Isabelline lily, clove carnations, mullein, lupine, hyacinth, red primrose, auricula, polyanthus, guelder rose, anemone, moss rose, scarlet lychnis, pink geranium (its leaves variegated with white), convolvulus, sunflower, sweet-william, scabious, and Canterbury bells, whence one is able to form a good notion of the furniture of a Scottish garden in the eighteenth century. Strange to say, the common daffodil is not among them ; the only representative of the family being that double form of *Narcissus incomparabilis* which goes by the homely name of Butter-and-eggs.

No doubt many of the flowers still adorning these grounds are borne on the same roots which furnished patterns for the gentle artist a century and a half ago ; for there is no fixed limit to the life of some of the humblest herbs. The oxlip may outlive the oak which overshadows it ; yonder massive sycamore may be but a child in years compared with the celandine that stars the bank at its foot, and who shall declare the "expectation of life" in the lowly stonecrop that creeps beneath our feet. The green mound, whereon stands the keep of the old castle, breaks out each spring on its south side with a constellation of white violets, wide-spread on the slope. They have long outlived the memory of

44

her who planted them, for it is more than a century since the castle was inhabited. On the terrace at Monreith there is planted in clipped box the Psalmist's note of warning—*Homo quasi flos egreditur et conteritur* ; but those who covet length of days might willingly exchange terms of life with "the hyssop that springeth out of the wall."

GARTINCABER

HE whole plan and purpose of this book being to illustrate types of Scottish horticulture, the grandiose and elaborate have received no preference over the unpretending and simple. Any space of Scottish soil, be its dimensions calculable in roods or in acres, will serve our turn, so that it be an abode of flowers well tended, or at least, unspoilt, by its owner.

Simple, indeed, is the garden design at Gartincaber—a plain rectangle sloping pleasantly to the sun ; at the upper-end a sixteenth century tower, with nineteenth century additions naively contrived ; at the lower-end a clear pool, not ample enough to aspire to the title of "loch," yet, shadowed by dark firs on the far side, too comely to bear the common Scottish term "a stank." This walled enclosure is laid out in the old manner, subdivided by crossed paths, with a sun-dial at the crossing ; kitchen herbs and small fruits in the four quarters,

46

GARTINCABER

GARTINCABER

HE whole plan and purpose of this book being to illustrate types of Scottish horticulture, the grandiose and elaborate have received no preference over the unpretending and simple. . . . . . . Scottish soil, be its dimensions calculated . . in acres, will serve our turn, ... of flowers well tended, or . . . its owner.

. . . the garden design at Gartin-. . . . angle sloping pleasantly to the . . . . end a sixteenth century tower, with . . . . century additions naively contrived; at the . . . a clear pool, not ample enough to a . . . . . le of "loch," yet, shadowed by dark . . . far side, too comely to bear the . . . . . term "a stank." This walled . . . . . in the old manner, subdivided . . crossed . . . with a sundial at the crossing; . . . . . small fruits in the four quarters,

46

GARTINCABER.

with narrow selvage of flowering things, overhung here and there by aged apple trees. Nothing can have been further from the designer's intention than landscape effect: use, not ornament, was his purpose, flowers being admitted in grudging concession to feminine frivolity ; but age has brought about delectable results—age, and the affectionate tending of generations. Lofty holly hedges, such as John Evelyn praised, screen the litter in such corners where litter must be ; a few massive sycamores add dignity to the scene in winter and shade from summer heat, without, as it seems, impoverishing the borders, for these teem with blossom to the very feet of the trees. But they are flowers of modest requirements—winter aconites and snowdrops, daffodils and wind-flowers, bloodroot, violets white and purple, primroses and oxlips of many hues—all old friends, the older the better to be loved. On this mid-April morning in a late—a very late—season, what strikes one as most notable is the abundance of double white primroses on usually long footstalks, surely a strain peculiar to the place.

I have dwelt on the simplicity of this garden, but every yard of it bears witness to affectionate care, and in one respect this affection has evinced itself in a manner reflecting agreeably the classical taste of a bygone age. Thus at the foot of the slope has been placed a wide stone bench, whereof the back bears this inscription :

47

SCOTTISH GARDENS

HORTO · QVEM · AMAMVS · HANC · SEDEM · DONAVIMVS
MARY · HANNAH · ANNE · ALICE
FILIÆ
IOHANNIS · ET · DOROTHEÆ · MVRDOCH
MDCCCCV.[1]

And again :

ILLE · TERRARVM · MIHI · PRÆTER · OMNES
ANGVLVS · RIDET.[2]

The sun-dial in the middle of the garden is also
inscribed with many legends, and bears on its base
a dedication to Mr. and Mrs. Burn-Murdoch "on
their golden wedding," from their grandchildren,
Lorna, Dorothea, Ian, Marion, and Colin.

It is no modern trait in the family, this pretty
taste for inscribing stones. During the four centuries
or thereby it has stood, the house of Gartincaber
has owned no other lord than a Murdoch, and the
dormer windows bear legends in relief ; on one,
NOSCE · TEIPSVM[3], surmounted by a thistle ; on another
a tag from *Juvenal* :

MORS · SOLA · FATETVR
QVANTVLA · SINT · HOMINVM · CORPVSCVLA,[4]

under a man with a bent bow.

---

[1] "Mary, Hannah, Anne, Alice, daughters of John and Dorothy Murdoch, have presented this seat to the garden which we love. 1905." *Horto nobis dilecto* had been a more graceful rendering.

[2] "This little corner pleases me better than all the world beside."
Horace, *Odes* ii. 6.

[3] "Know thyself"—the Attic γνῶθι σεαυτόν. "Oh Athenians, your wisdom reaches us across the centuries! We hear your murmured messages—'Know thyself,' 'Nothing in excess!' We who have travelled so far, and yet so little, we who are still scaling the heights you reached—Athenians, we salute you!"
The Diary of a Looker-on, by C. Lewis Hind.

[4] "Death alone discloses how feeble are the bodies of men."—Juvenal, *Sat.* x, 173.

48

GARTINCABER

Again :

TECVM · HABITA · ET · NORIS · QVAM · SIT · TIBI · CVRTA · SVPELLEX.[1]

The following sentiment :

CONVIVAM · CAVEO · QVI · SE · MIHI · COMPARAT · ET · RES
DESPICIT EXIGVAS,[2]

may have been inspired by the haughtiness of some affluent neighbour ; the lord of Doune, perhaps, whose great castle, though now in ruins, still scowls defiance from the further shore of Teith.

Even the latest addition to the old house bears its appropriate legend, the gable of the new drawing-room bearing one well expressing the spirit which has attached this family to its ancient home :

I · DWELL · AMONG · MY · OWN · PEOPLE.[3]

Of the two avenues which, planted at right angles to each other, lead up to the house, the northern, consisting of two double rows of beeches, has been sorely wrecked by gales, but the west avenue is still intact, a remarkable and far-seen feature in the landscape. Running along the comb of a ridge, it is composed of lime trees which appear to be about 100 or 120 years old. The two rows are only fifteen feet apart ; and the trees, set very closely in the rows, have been drawn up to the height of a hundred feet. There is no nobler prospect in Scotland, none richer in historic association, than

---

[1] "Live by yourself, and you will find out how ill-furnished is your mind."— Persius, iv. 52.

[2] "I am on my guard against the guest who draws comparisons between himself and me, and contemns my slender means."

[3] 2 Kings iv. 13.

that commanded from the outer end of this avenue. Yon white tower, standing in the newly sown cornland, was built to mark the centre of the Scottish realm; broad and fair around it spreads the fertile carse, through which the looped Forth winds its leisurely way. You may trace its gleams till they are lost in the blue haze on the east, where the sunlit Ochils, Stirling Castle, and Polmaise woods arrest the eye, only a little nearer than blood-boultered Bannockburn and Falkirk. All along the southern horizon stretch the flat-topped Lennox Hills and Campsie Fells, their outline presenting marked contrast to the tumultuous range on the north, where Ben Ledi and Stuc-a'chroin still wear their snowy hoods. Far on the west Ben Lomond rears its cloven cone, commanding outpost of the Highland host. Every feature in the landscape has its story for the understanding eye, from northward Ardoch, where Julius Agricola has left enduring memorial of his conquest in the earthen ramparts of his camp, to nearer Kippen on the south, where Prince Charlie's Highlanders crossed the Ford of Frew when last Great Britain felt the throes of civil strife.

A word about the Murdochs of Gartincaber. They trace their descent from one Murdoch, who rendered yeoman service to Robert the Bruce in his hour of need. In the early spring of 1307, the King of Scots was hiding in the Galloway hill country with a few hundred followers. King Edward's troops beset all the passes: escape seemed impossible, and Bruce caused his men to separate into small companies, so as to make subsistence easier. But he appointed a day when they were all to muster at the hill now called Craigencallie, on the eastern shore of lonely Loch Dee. Here, in a solitary cabin, dwelt a widow,[1] the mother of three sons, each by a different husband, and named Murdoch, Mackie and MacLurg.

The King arrived first, and alone, at the rendezvous. Weary and half-famished, he asked the widow for some food; nor asked in vain, for, said she, all wayfarers are welcome for the sake of *one*. "And who may that one be?" asked the King.— "None other than Robert the Bruce," quoth the goodwife, "rightful lord of this land, wha e'er gainsays it. He's hard pressed just now, but he'll come by his own, sure enough."

This was good hearing for the King, who made himself known at once, was taken into the house and sat down to the best meal he had eaten for many days. While he was so employed, the three sons returned, whose mother straightway made them do obeisance to their liege lord. They declared their readiness to enter his service at once, but the King would put their prowess as marksmen to the test before engaging them. Two ravens sat together on a crag a bowshot off; the eldest son, Murdoch, let fly at them and transfixed both with one

---

[1] The name Craigencallie signifies in Gaelic " the old woman's crag," and is cited in evidence of the truth of the legend.

arrow. Next, Mackie shot at a raven flying over-head, and brought it to the ground, and the King was satisfied, although poor MacLurg missed his mark altogether.

In after years, when the widow's words had been fulfilled by Bruce coming to his own and being acknow-ledged King of Scots, he sent for the widow and asked her to name the reward she had earned by her timely hospitality.

" Just gie me," said she, " yon wee bit hassock o' land that lies atween Palnure and Penkiln "—two streams flowing into Wigtown Bay.

The King granted her request. The " bit hassock," being about five miles long and three broad, was divided between the three sons, from whom descended the families of Murdoch of Cumloden, Mackie of Larg, and MacLurg of Kirouchtrie. Cumloden re-mained the property of the family of Murdoch till 1738, when it was sold to the Earl of Galloway to discharge an accumulation of debt. The fine shooting of the founder of the family is com-memorated in the arms borne by his descendants, and duly enrolled in the Lyon Register, viz., *Argent*, two ravens hanging palewise, *sable*, with an arrow through both their heads fess-wise, *proper*.

In the Justiciary Records of Scotland there is brief record of a horrible outrage perpetrated upon Patrick Murdoch of Cumloden in 1605. Robert and John, sons of Peter M'Dowall of Machermore, a near neighbour of Cumloden, were arraigned upon a charge of having seized Murdoch and his servant Peter M'Kie, and cut off their right hands. Peter M'Dowall was accepted as surety for his sons, who were liberated on their father's undertaking that they would appear for trial at Kirkcudbright, after receiving fifteen days' notice. But the M'Dowalls were a powerful clan. When the case was called at the assizes, a jury could not be empannelled, twenty-seven persons who were summoned preferring to pay the statutory fine rather than serve ; and we hear no more either of the malefactors or their victims.

PRINCES STREET GARDENS

EDINBURGH

RAVELLERS have been heard to utter unkind things about the climate of Edinburgh, which has been much the same, I suppose, for the last thousand years; and those who have not visited the city may have been deterred from doing so by its by-name of "Auld Reekie," which its inhabitants do not resent, albeit that of the "Modern Athens" may be more alluring. In truth, both the climate and the atmosphere are compatible with horticulture of a very high class; for the first is no worse than the rest of the east coast, where there is no dearth of fruits and of flowers, and the second is singularly free from smoke for a town of 317,459 inhabitants. Edinburgh earned its name of Auld Reekie from no internal murkiness; it was conferred by a famous golfer of the eighteenth century, James Durham of Largo, who, from his home in Fife, used to watch the chimneys of the capital, and, as Robert Chambers records, "was in the habit of regulating the time of evening worship by the appearance of the smoke of Edinburgh. When it increased in density, in conse-

PRINCES STREET GARDENS

EDINBURGH

have been heard to utter
gs about the climate of
which has been much the
pose, for the last thousand
those who have not visited
the may have been deterred from doing so by its
of "Auld Reekie" which its inhabitants do
that the "Modern Athens" may
uth, both the climate and the
are ible with horticulture of a very
irst is no worse than the rest
here there is no dearth of fruits
the second is singularly free from
oke n of 317,459 inhabitants. Edinburgh
earned of Auld Reekie from no internal
murk was conferred by a famous golfer of
the entury, James Durham of Largo,
from ome in Fife, used to watch the
chimneys of the capital, and, as Robert Chambers
words, "was the habit of regulating the time of
evening worship by the appearance of the smoke of
Edinburgh. When it increased in density, in conse-

54

PRINCES STREET GARDENS, EDINBURGH.

quence of the good folk preparing supper, he would say, 'It is time, noo, bairns, to tak the buiks and gang to our beds, for yonder's Auld Reekie, I see, putting on her nightcap.'" And the nickname was confirmed and made irrevocable by a later and greater authority than James Durham. "Yonder stands Auld Reekie," says Adam Woodcock to young Roland Græme, "you may see the smoke hover over her at twenty miles distant, as the goshawk hangs over a plump of young wild ducks."[1]

Of fresh air and light there is no lack in modern Edinburgh. One longs to bring back Sir William Brereton, were it but to cause him to recant the harsh judgment he passed upon the city in 1636.

"The sluttishness and nastiness of this people is such that I cannot omit the particularizing thereof. . . their houses and halls and kitchens have such a noisome taste, a savour, and that so strong, as it doth offend you so soon as you come within their wall; yea, sometimes when I have light from my horse, I have felt the distaste of it before I have come into my house; yea, I never came to my own lodging in Edinburgh, or went out, but I was constrained to hold my nose, or to use wormwood, or some such scented plant."

Much more and worse has this stern old Puritan to reproach the sanitation of Edinburgh withal; but that was more than two centuries before Sir Henry Littlejohn appeared on the scene.[2]

[1] *The Abbot*, chap. xvii.

[2] Sir Henry was chief sanitary authority in the city for forty-six years, retiring under the Civil Service age regulations in 1906 with a remarkable record of good work to his credit, and, it is to be hoped, many years of well-earned repose before him.

SCOTTISH GARDENS

The series of Scottish garden types would be far from complete if it did not include a town garden, and certain it is that we Scots owe much gratitude to the municipal rulers of our metropolis for the admirable manner in which the ground along the south side of Princes Street is beautified. Miss Wilson's view is taken in the eastern garden, between the Doric temple on the Mound, upon which John Ruskin erewhile discharged the fluent vials of his wrath, and the great monument which, perhaps, owes its magnificence even more to the degree in which Sir Walter Scott's personal character endeared him to his countrymen as a man than to their recognition of his accomplishment as a poet. Adam Black, founder of the well-known firm of publishers, undoubtedly deserved well of his fellow-citizens, for he was twice Lord Provost of Edinburgh, and worthily represented that city in Parliament ; but when they resolved to commemorate him they acted somewhat unkindly in erecting his statue in such near proximity to the canopy which soars over the homely figure of "the Shirra," and practically eclipses the lesser monument.

Impressively beautiful as she is in a degree beyond any other city in the British Isles, Edinburgh might have become still more so had men foreseen what modern methods of sanitation have rendered possible. When the city wall was razed after the middle of the eighteenth century, before the New Town had come into existence, the hollow between the Old

PRINCES STREET GARDENS

Town and Princes Street was occupied by the Nor'
Loch, a sheet of water which formed an important
part of the military defences of the city, but
which we may well imagine had become the offensive
receptacle of the waste products of a growing population. Accordingly it was drained away, and a
matchless opportunity for landscape gardening was
lost for ever. Still, the great glen remained, capable
of conversion into a green valley with pleasant groves ;
but all this was irremediably marred when, in 1844,
the North British Railway was driven through the
old bed of the loch, filling all the air with smoke
and dreadful noise.

Down to this time, the eastern part of this
ground had been let to a nurseryman or market-
gardener ; but the Town Council now resumed possession, building the terraces and parapets and forming
the walks which complete the design of the Scott
memorial. More and more care and money was
applied to the adornment of what became known as
East Princes Street Gardens, until, under the administration of Mr. John M'Hattie, they now present
a really remarkable example of spring and summer
gardening in the formal manner. All the greater
credit is due to Mr. M'Hattie and his.staff for this
result because of the stormy position which these
gardens occupy, fully exposed to the pitiless easterly
gales which blow in from the North Sea with relentless persistency.

Miss Wilson's study was made in spring when

tulips and wall-flowers display their vigorous hues. The effect is softer in summer, when the tints blend with gentler gradation, but in autumn the borders flame out again with a blaze of chrysanthemums, carrying one well into the dark days which intervene before the coming of the crocuses.

In 1876 the Corporation acquired the West Princes Street Gardens, hitherto reserved for the proprietors of houses *ex adverso*. These grounds are of very great extent, lying right up to the foot of the Castle Rock, and, although bisected by the broad railroad, have been converted into a veritable pleasaunce, less formal in manner than the East Gardens. Under Mr. M'Hattie's care, great improvements have been effected; hardy trees, shrubs, and herbs have been liberally planted, and many borders are devoted to spring and summer bedding. Warmly must the Corporation and their servants be congratulated on the result of their enterprise. They have turned the land at their disposal to the very best account, and created a brilliant foreground to the Old Town and the Castle such as those who remember Princes Street Gardens forty years ago could never have anticipated. We can only sigh after the departed Nor' Loch when we reflect what a feature it might have been made when purified and committed to Mr. M'Hattie's skilful hands to work into his landscape.

BABERTON

MIDLOTHIAN

ABERTON is a typical example of the kind of country residence erected in the eighteenth century by professional men whose business lay in the metropolis at a time when all classes in Scotland were beginning to feel the beneficial effects of the legislative union between the richer and the poorer realm. Whether that be the origin of this pretty demesne or not, I know not for certain, having had access to no records of the past of Baberton; but the house, viewed from outside, appears to be of the date indicated, with some pleasing architectural features characterising that period. Since its foundation, Edinburgh has spread far beyond her pristine limits, and the district has become thoroughly suburban; but the owners of Baberton have managed to keep their neighbours at ample distance; only a golf course impinges upon the south side of their demesne, which remains a silvan oasis in the surrounding labyrinth of villadom.

The garden lies within walls in the fold of a

59

shallow glen, forming two wings divided by a central wall. The northernmost wing, sloping fairly to the south, is just a herb garden in the old Scottish manner, with aged apple trees, grass alleys and borders well filled with summer flowers.

In the southern wing, the buttresses of the outer wall supply a pretty feature, of which advantage has been taken to establish thereon stonecrop and saxifrage. From this a steep rustic path descends into the hollow, which Miss Wilson has depicted in its vernal brightness, with a glimpse of the more formal garden beyond. There is also some well-constructed rock-work on the steep bank, whereon a small collection of alpine plants are thriving satisfactorily. The whole enclosure appears not to exceed an acre in extent, but careful cultivation and discriminating care have rendered it far more beautiful and interesting than many more ambitious and extensive gardens.

BABERTON.

POLLOK

N the year of grace 1270 or thereabouts Sir Aymer Maxwell of Caerlaverock granted to his third son, Sir John Maxwell, the lands of Nether Pollok in the county of Renfrew, from whom the present owner, Sir John Stirling Maxwell, is twenty-third in direct descent, through his grand-mother, who married Archibald Stirling of Keir. Six hundred and thirty-seven years have wrought much change in nearly every part of King Edward's realm, but nowhere has the landscape undergone more wholesale metamorphosis within a like period than in the valley of the White Cart.

When Sir John Maxwell took possession of his estate in the thirteenth century, Glasgow was a modest hamlet, clustering round the brand-new cathedral of Bishop Joceline; it has now overflowed upon 11,861 acres on both banks of the Clyde, which winds through the municipal area for a distance of five miles and a half.

It is not only the land surface which has altered

61

in appearance, forest and crag making way for closely packed dwellings and factories; the Clyde and its lower tributaries were allowed to become so foully polluted that a lifeless, evil-smelling current flows where once the silvery salmon thronged up from the firth and innumerable water-fowl flocked for food. That is in process of being remedied by a painstaking municipality; but who shall purge the sky of the smoke rising from the hearths of 780,000 inhabitants and the reek belched from a thousand factory chimneys and gas-works?

Nor is that all that must be reckoned. In a wide circle round Glasgow have arisen police-burghs—Kinning Park, Govan, Partick, Pollokshaws, Cathcart, etc.—each with a population exceeding that of many a mediæval city, each with its smoke-producing industries, and only a little further afield is Paisley with 87,000 inhabitants, Johnstone with 12,000, Port-Glasgow with 18,000, Greenock with 68,000, all combining to darken the air; and, as though that were not enough to discourage horticulture, all the land unbuilt on is threaded with railways, honeycombed with coal-pits, studded with smelting furnaces, pouring forth volumes of smoke night and day. So it has come to pass that from whatever quarter the wind sets, it is charged with the products of combustion—in other words, with coal smoke.

This, as every forester, gardener and amateur can testify, is a relentless foe to almost every kind of vegetable life. Strange to say, mosses and lichens, humblest in the scale, succumb first, so that in all this region stones and tree stems are devoid of that kindly covering which always gathers upon them in a pure atmosphere. The next to suffer are trees themselves; for although many fine elms, beeches, oaks, sycamores, ash, and even pines survive in this wide strath, these grew to maturity under conditions very different from those now prevailing, and the growth of young trees, especially conifers and oaks, is sorely checked and blighted by carbon deposit and sulphurous fumes.

Nevertheless, horticulture dies hard; the instinct of every man owning a garden is to obey the primæval command "to dress it and to keep it"; and Miss Wilson has chosen a scene in the garden at Pollok as an example of what combined skill and resolution may accomplish in the most forbidding environment.

The subject of the picture is a terrace wall, constructed only five or six years ago of ashlar masonry, with slits purposely left between some of the joints for the insertion of suitable flowering plants.

The park of Pollok is but a green oasis round which Glasgow and the neighbouring burghs have flowed like a dark and rapidly rising tide. Yet here, on this terrace wall, within constant sound of steam hooters and whistles, steam hammers and pumps, you may see alpine flowers blooming as profusely and with colours as clear as they do on the loftiest solitudes on earth and in the purest atmosphere.

63

SCOTTISH GARDENS

The chief display when this picture was painted—in May—came from the varieties of *Aubrietia* with their hanging cushions of purple and mauve, and golden *Alyssum*. Common things, these, yet priceless in their effect and unfailing in the reward they make for attention to their simple wants. A month later, the purple and gold had been dimmed; a rose-coloured mist had spread along the wall, created by different kinds of dwarf *Dianthus* and *Silene*, with the common sea-thrift of our shores; while through the mist shone stars of *Arenaria* and many species of saxifrage and stonecrop. Dwarf bell flowers, also, spread blue curtains over the stones, among the most effective being the glaucous variety of *Campanula garganica*, known as *hirsuta, C. pusilla* and the hybrid "G. F. Wilson," *C. muralis*, which must now be sought for under the preposterous title of *C. portenschlageana*.

All these are anybody's flowers, anybody's, that is, who has the wit to raise them from seed, for they are not particular as to soil (though most of them show gratitude for an admixture and occasional top-dressing of old lime rubbish), or climate, as their luxuriance in this Glasgow atmosphere amply testifies. But among these commoner things are herbs, if not of greater beauty, of greater rarity. Specially to be commended are the little Himalayan *Potentilla nitida*, with silvery leaves and delicate flesh-coloured flowers, like miniature Tudor roses; *Myosotis rupicola*, an exquisite forget-me-not which likes to be wedged tightly into a rock crevice; our native purple saxifrage

S. oppositifolia, the golden-flowered *S. sancta* from far Mount Athos, the fragrant *S. apiculata*, thickly set with panicles of sulphur-coloured blossoms, exactly the hue of a wild primrose, in early spring; and, earliest and finest of all, the snowy-petalled *S. Burseriana*. Then the encrusted section of rock-foils, bewildering in variety, delight in such a position, growing into such exquisite bosses and wreaths that one almost grudges the profusion of their bloom, which conceals the delicate carving of their foliage.

It is wonderful how readily these and other mountaineers adapt themselves to their unpromising environment. The truth is that, like the red deer, they have taken to the mountain tops because they have been crowded out of the low country, where they were overwhelmed in competition with other herbs; so they survive only in places where their constitution enables them to endure conditions unfavourable to rank vegetation. A notable and oft-quoted example of this is the common thrift, which is found all round our coasts at sea level and on the summits of some of our highest mountains, both these situations being unfavourable to the majority of lowland vegetation; but one may search in vain for a single specimen of thrift between these two extremes. That it would thrive anywhere is proved by the ease with which it may be cultivated in gardens at any level; cultivation, in this instance, amounting to no more than the suppression of competing vegetation.

SCOTTISH GARDENS

In planting a terrace wall like that at Pollok it is necessary to raise seedlings or cuttings which may be inserted while still small in the crevices of the masonry. After being settled in their places they drive their roots to almost incredible distance into the solid earth behind the wall, which protects them alike from summer drought and trying variations of temperature in winter, while the vertical surface ensures rapid drainage and protection from frost.

The narrow border at the wall-foot provides a congenial home for choice bulbous and other plants, which, if carefully selected, may keep up a continuous display almost throughout the year. The list of suitable plants for this purpose might be made a long one. The following one contains suggestion for a small collection which may be added to at pleasure, suitable for a northerly climate.

December to March—

    Iris reticulata and *persica.*
    Cyclamen coum and *vernum.*
    Eranthis hyemalis.
    Hepaticas in variety.
    Adonis amurensis.

March and April—

    Scilla sibirica, amœna and *bifolia.*
    Chionodoxa Luciliœ and *Sardensis.*
    Narcissus minor and other dwarf daffodils.
    Crocus in variety.
    Erica carnea.

POLLOK.

POLLOK

Anemone blanda.
Callianthemum rutæfolium.
Erythronium in variety.
Muscari Szovitzianum and other choice species.
Fritillaria aurea.
Tulipa pulchella, Lownii, saxatilis, etc.
Sisyrinchium grandiflorum.
Primula rosea and *denticulata.*

May and June—
Tulipa Greigi, linifolia, etc.
Daphne Cneorum and *Blageana.*
Muscari "Heavenly Blue."
Sanguinaria canadensis.
Anemone nemorosa var. Robinsoniana.
Incarvillea grandiflora.
Hyacinthus amethystinus.
Ranunculus amplexicaulis.
Scilla verna.
Nierembergia rivularis.
Polygonum sphærocephalum.
Delphinium nudicaule.
Ornithogalum nutans.
Iris pumila and other dwarf species.
Primula luteola, sikkimensis, etc.

July and August—
Hypericum fragile and *reptans.*
Gaultheria trichomanes.
Allium pedemontanum and other choice dwarf
    species.
Erica Maweana.

SCOTTISH GARDENS

Andromeda polifolia.
Anomatheca cruenta.
Primula capitata.

September and October—
Colchicum speciosum and other choice species.
Crocus speciosus and other choice species.
Polygonum vaccinifolium.
Cyclamen europæum and *libanoticum.*
Cornus canadensis.

November and December—
Schizostylus coccineus.
Helleborus altifolius.
Primroses, garden varieties.

STONEFIELD

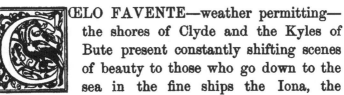ŒLO FAVENTE—weather permitting—
the shores of Clyde and the Kyles of
Bute present constantly shifting scenes
of beauty to those who go down to the
sea in the fine ships the Iona, the
Columba or the Grenadier; but of the many thousands
who take their pleasure in this way every summer,
what a small percentage suspect what treasures are
stored in the sloping woods on either hand. No
English gardener will believe, till he has seen for
himself, what luxuriant growth of tender exotics can
be produced on the west coast of Scotland, wherever
it is possible to provide shelter from Atlantic gales.
The fierce winds and mighty rollers that waste their
fury for weeks together on the rock-bound western
isles, can work no ruin in the long, narrow fjords
which intersect the mainland. I was prepared, therefore, to find evidence of a very gentle climate along
the shores of Loch Fyne; but what I found exceeded
all anticipation.

If you look at the map of Argyll, you will see

that the promontory of Cantyre, a finger of land
about forty miles long and, on an average, not more
than seven miles wide, only escapes severance from
the mainland by means of a strip of ground a mile
wide. When Malcolm Canmore ceded to Magnus
Barefoot, King of Norway, all the islands "between
which and the mainland he could pass in a galley
with its rudder shipped," the Northman secured
Cantyre by running his craft ashore at the head
of West Loch Tarbert, and causing it to be drawn
on rollers across the isthmus to Loch Fyne, with his
own hand on the tiller. Three hundred years later,
Robert the Bruce repeated the feat, in token of his
lordship of the Isles, and built a keep at the eastern
end of the portage, which still presides, grim and
time-worn, over the snug little town of Tarbert, with
its tortuous, but profound, harbour. These incidents
are commemorated in the name of the place, Tarbert
signifying "boat draft" or portage, from the Gaelic
taruinn bada.

North of the isthmus lies the district of Knapdale,
near the southern extremity of which is Mr. George
Campbell's fine demesne of Stonefield, facing the blue
waters of Loch Fyne on the east and sheltered from
prevailing winds by high ground on the south-west
and north-west. To enumerate half the rare forms
of vegetation which thrive among the ample woodland
of Stonefield would fill a very long chapter. Readers
will kindly be content with the bare notes of a visit
paid to these grounds in mid-April.

STONEFIELD

STONEFIELD

The first things to attract attention are some specimens of *Eucalyptus gunni*, the tallest of which is 80 feet high, and 5 feet in circumference at 4 feet from the ground, with a beautiful clean bole of 25 feet. The blue gum (*E. globulus*), though perfectly hardy against frost, grows such length of soft wood that it constantly gets broken by the wind. Probably if planted in mass, the trees would protect each other, but *E. gunni* is evidently a preferable species.

Near the foot of one of these gum-trees is a bush of the Chilian *Desfontainea spinosa*, a mass of rich myrtle green, 75 feet in circumference and 14 feet high. It has been severely cut in on one side, to prevent it overspreading a gravel path, and, when thickly set with its scarlet and yellow blossoms, must indeed be "a sight for sair e'en." Another shrub, from the southern hemisphere, *Griselinia littoralis* from New Zealand, here assumes the proportions of a small tree, 30 feet high. *Mitraria coccinea*, seldom seen in British gardens, and, when seen, usually of very modest dimensions, has grown so dense and spread so wide that last year a hen pheasant chose a bush of it for her nesting place. *Philesia buxifolia* rivals it in size; *Abutilon vitifolium*, 15 feet high, *Myrtus (Eugenia) apiculata* and *Cordyline Australis* each 20 feet high, *Escallonia rubra* with a stem girth of 2 feet, *Buddleia Colvillei* 9 feet high, are a few of the things most worth noting before passing on to examine the rhododendrons, which are the special glory of the place. By the by, why can we not drop that cumbrous polysyllable and adopt the American name "rose bay" or "rose laurel"?

The presence of these fine plants dates from the 'forties, when Sir Joseph Hooker, with youthful ardour, was revelling in the floral wealth of the Himalayas. Dr. Campbell, of the family of Oronsay, who founded the sanatorium of Darjeeling in 1835, shared Hooker's enthusiasm, and sent home quantities of seed, some of which found its way to Stonefield. A noble crop has sprung from it. Here are trees of *Rhododendron arboreum* 30 feet high with blood-red, pink or white blossoms, and with stems thicker than any wood-nymph's waist; *R. Falconeri* 25 feet high, carrying among its great felted leaves between 200 and 300 trusses of waxy bells; *R. eximium*, probably a local variety of the last-named, loaded with bloom; *R. barbatum*, the bearded rose-bay, in both varieties, one a month later in bloom than the other, both excelling all their kind in the glow of blood-red flowers. *R. Thomsoni* stands 15 feet high and 20 feet in diameter, and among other treasures may be mentioned *Rhododendron grande* (*argenteum*), a shy flowerer, but worth growing for its splendid foliage alone; *R. niveum* with purple flowers and leaves lined with white *peau de Suède R. Hodgsoni* with leaves like *Falconeri* but with rosy flowers, *R. fragrantissimum*, *campanulatum* and *ciliatum*, all revelling in conditions of season and temperature as unlike their native levels of from 8000 to 12,000 feet as one could well imagine. In the Himalayas, all growth is restrained until late in spring, when it is suddenly released for a summer burst, and as suddenly brought to a stop for a long winter rest; whereas in the West Highlands of Scotland there is no such demarcation of seasons; growth is encouraged from year's end to year's end, subject to sharp snaps at uncertain intervals. It is truly remarkable how well these fine plants accommodate themselves to every trial except that of rude winds.

Perhaps the most distinguished, because the rarest, of the rhododendrons which were in flower at the time of my visit was *R. campylocarpum*, 9 feet high, bearing trusses of beautiful waxy bells, clear canary yellow with a purple stain at the base of each bell.

CASTLE KENNEDY

WIGTOWNSHIRE

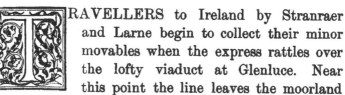RAVELLERS to Ireland by Stranraer and Larne begin to collect their minor movables when the express rattles over the lofty viaduct at Glenluce. Near this point the line leaves the moorland through which it runs almost continuously for forty miles westward of Castle Douglas, and enters upon a flat cultivated tract. Glimpses of the sea, which at no distant geological period covered this plain, may be had on either hand; Loch Ryan forming the northern, as Luce Bay the southern, horizon.

At the narrowest part of the isthmus between these seas a liberal space has been devoted to landscape gardening on a heroic scale. On the right of the railway, three or four miles east of Stranraer, the traveller may view the ample demesne, or (to use the native phrase) the "policies" of Castle Kennedy; and, if he is master of his own time, will do well to devote a morning to closer inspection thereof.

CASTLE KENNEDY.

CASTLE KENNEDY

If there is a prevailing blemish in British park scenery, it is a tendency to sameness. That has been avoided at Castle Kennedy by a peculiar treatment of natural features, in themselves the reverse of imposing, such as I have not seen attempted on a similar scale elsewhere. Here, on the isthmus between two seas, lie two ample sheets of fresh water, the Black and the White Lochs of Inch ; and the inner isthmus between these lakes has been wrought into a strange complexity of terraces and grassy slopes. The ruins of Castle Kennedy, a good example of the domestic architecture of the seventeenth century, destroyed by fire in 1715, stand on a green plateau at one end of this isthmus. At the other end, best part of a mile distant, is the modern mansion of Lochinch, residence of the Earl of Stair, a spacious specimen of that style which was developed under French influence in the sixteenth century ; when country houses, ceasing to be purely defensive, assumed more hospitable features.

How comes it that two such great castles stand fronting each other within the same demesne ? Was it not said by those of olden time, and have not our fathers declared unto us, that—

> " 'Twixt Wigtown and the town of Ayr,
> Portpatrick and the Cruives o' Cree,
> Nae man need think for to bide there
> Except he ride wi' Kennedy."

SCOTTISH GARDENS

Ah! but time brings strange revenges. About ten miles east of Castle Kennedy, on a bleak and boggy moorland, are the ruins of Carscreuch; a mansion whereof Symson, the seventeenth century chronicler of this district, drily observes that it "might have been more pleasant if it had been in a more pleasant place." This most ineligible residence, shortly after Symson described it, passed by marriage into possession of Sir James Dalrymple, first Viscount Stair. Some three hundred years previously, the Kennedy clan had violently despoiled the Dalrymples of their modest possessions in Ayrshire, accomplishing that purpose not without much arson and bloodshed. The turn of the Dalrymples came when the seventh Earl of Cassilis, chief of the Kennedys, floundered into innumerable scrapes in covenanting times. Generation after generation, the Dalrymples were serviceable lawyers. Acre by acre, farm by farm, the wide lands of Kennedy in Wigtownshire passed to that family which owns them at this day.

This first Viscount Stair, President of the Court of Session, had a daughter Janet, out of whose troubled fortunes Scott created Lucy Ashton, the Bride of Lammermoor. The father of the seventh Earl of Cassilis, who, as aforesaid, was forced to part with his territory to his hereditary enemy, also figures in Scottish romance, for his first wife's elopement furnished a theme for the well-known ballad of *Johnnie Faa*.

CASTLE KENNEDY

"The gypsies cam' to our lord's yett,
  And O but they sang sweetly;
They sang sae sweet and sae very complete
  That down came the fair lady.

And she cam' tripping doun the stair,
  And a' her maids before her;
As sune as they saw her weel-faured face,
  They cuist their glamour o'er her.

'O come wi' me,' says Johnnie Faa,
  'O come wi' me, my dearie;
For I vow and I swear by the hilt o' my sword
  That your lord shall nae mair come near ye.'

  .   .   .   .   .   .

'Gae tak' frae me this gay mantle,
  And bring to me a plaidie;
For if kith and kin and a' had sworn,
  I'll follow the gypsy laddie.

'Yestreen I lay in a weel-made bed,
  Wi' my gude lord beside me;
This night I'll lie in a tenant's barn,
  Whatever shall betide me!'"[1]

It was John second Earl of Stair, better known
as Field-Marshal Stair, who, in the interval between
his military and diplomatic achievements, planned

---

[1] It is only fair to the memory of this countess, who was Lady Jean Hamilton, daughter of the first Earl of Haddington, that the legend of her elopement is amply disproved by the fact that she lived with her husband for 21 years, and that he spoke of her with much affection in letters written after her death. W. E. Aytoun carefully examined the character of this ballad, which he regarded as "by far the most mysterious of Scottish traditionary tales," and failed to reconcile it with any real incident. In publishing it in his *Ballads of Scotland*, he suggested that it "was a malignant fiction, possibly trumped up to annoy Bishop Burnet (who married Lady Cassilis's daughter) who had many enemies."

the terraces and pleasure grounds of Castle Kennedy,
and embellished his lands with much planting. The
work lasted from 1730 to 1740 under direction of one
Thomas M'Alla, from whose copious correspondence
with his employer a couple of extracts may be permitted, were it only as an example of eighteenth
century orthography.

Castle Kennedy January y' 29th 1737.

I reciued your lordship's leter which giues me great
incuredgement to be kerfull and Diligent about what of your
lordsheps business I am Intrusted with, the principall work
nou in hand is that great walk alongs the Canall. Your lordshep
in the leter I got told me ther uas six troup horses to stand
at this ples In the Stabell to asist me in Carin on the work
they bing mothereth [moderate] wrought uold ben mor the
beter than uors [worse] and the work uold aduanced much
quiker but ther is non of them Com her as yet, they bing so
long Delied [delayed] and the Riding Exerces shortly coming
on I fer I will be littl the beter of them. I haue ben Remouing
the tris out of the gret land belo the bellvadair It will teak
a good deall of work but I sie by what Is don of It that it
will beutifi that pleace mor then what I could conceue from the
belluadair [belvedere] the bason apers lik a great glas . . . I
humbly thank your lordshep for the gret Incuregen leter I got
It was very Inlivening and reuiuing to me.

The "troup horses" referred to belonged to the
Scots Greys, of which famous regiment the Field-
Marshal was Colonel, and had a squadron thereof
permanently quartered in Wigtownshire. Five years
later, honest M'Alla was in difficulties, not for want of
horses but of that which "makes the mare to go."

78

CASTLE KENNEDY

Jan^r ye 5th 1738.

... I an nou diging the ground to Inlarge the planting at baluadair [Belvidere] as your lordship ordered. I am also Remouing that strip of planten on the uest sid of the flourin sherub wildernes the Alterations that uas med the last year and this on both sids of the flouring sherub wildernes, and the perter [parterre] beutifais that sid to perfection from Mount Malbarou to Mount Eliner; ther can be no finer prospect then it is nou ... I haue planted a lin of uery good bich [beech] at the foot of the bre [brae]. I was obledged to fors Earth to plant in them, for ther is no Earth in that bre; it is a lous dry runin sand. Ther is no tri uill grou on the fac of that bre, it bing so lous dray sand, without any mixter of Earth. .... Your lordshep desirs me to giue som money to the masons hir, but I ashour your lordshep I haue not on peny to my self. Your lordshep ordered Mr. Roos to giue me tuenty pound of my by gon uages, but he uold not giue me on farthen. I am uery sor straitened for som money I am deu to som pipell hir causes me nou to aplay to your lordshep for rellif. I thank God I haue your lordshep to aply to; I sie hou it uold be with me uer it otheruays."

Non sibi sed posteris. Upon no human undertaking does the decree *sic vos non vobis* attend so inevitably as upon tree planting. Scarcely had the Marshal's oaks cast their foliage a hundred times before a ruthless edict of the seventh Earl, known and dreaded by country folk as Hobblin' Jock, owing to a limp in his gait, laid every stick of them low, and the pleasure grounds went back to wilderness. The eighth Earl of Stair, succeeding in 1840, found a plan of the grounds in a gardener's cottage, and set to work to restore them. They were maintained and greatly beautified by his successors, especially by the tenth Earl, who died in 1903 at the age of 84. It is to his assiduous care that the present generation owes the fine collection of exotic conifers, broad-leaved trees and flowering shrubs. The landscape now only lacks what is held in store for generations unborn—the grace of aged timber—to fulfil the ideal of a lordly chace.

A great part of the isthmus between the lakes is devoted to a pinetum. Favoured by the mild western air, the Californian *Pinus insignis* (or *radiata*, Sargent) forms great domes of velvety bottle green, and the feathery Monterèy cypress (*C. macrocarpa*) grows as freely beside it as both do on the Pacific sea-board near San Francisco. Unluckily the gales which sweep across the broad lake on the west have wrought sore destruction among some of the firs. The Blue Avenue, for instance, as Sir Joseph Hooker named a double line of *Abies nobilis* on the slope facing the new castle, has been sadly knocked about, and the severe thinning practised in order to produce what are termed specimens has had the opposite result in many cases. Pines and firs are creatures of company, only displaying their special character of lofty, straight growth when they are disciplined as a forest. Yet there are growths of great beauty in the more sheltered places. The Himalayan *Cupressus torulosa*,[1] tolerant only of British climate in the mildest dis-

[1] Dr. Augustine Henry pronounces this specimen to be *Dacridium Franklinii.*

80

tricts, attracts attention from every arboriculturist.
A double avenue of Auracarias shows how much
these archaic trees gain by company of their own
kind; or, rather, how much they lose by being
isolated. Self-sown seedlings spring up freely under
these monkey-puzzles; other conifers which propagate
themselves very readily, where ground game does not
come, are *Abies nobilis* and *Webbiana.*

But after all, our concern is more with the
garden and flowering things than with forest trees.
Miss Wilson has planted her easel where the two
are inextricably blended, a bank of azaleas backed
by some aged evergreen oaks, which, by a lucky
chance, escaped the doom prepared for the rest of
the woodland by Hobblin' Jock. The water in the
foreground is M'Alla's "bason lik a great glas."

The most remarkable feature, however, at Castle
Kennedy is the vast number of choice rhododendrons,
including many that are not usually reckoned
hardy. There are hundreds of *R. arboreum,*
cinnamomeum and *campanulatum,* chiefly white and
pale-tinted, with which the glorious scarlet of *R.*
barbatum and *Thomsoni* contrasts with almost startling
effect. Rose and carmine are supplied by other
varieties of *R. arboreum* and by its hybrids, while
R. niveum supplies a note of deep mauve, with
which, later in the season, one's eye is apt to be
surfeited when the common *R. ponticum* is in bloom.
To see this matchless display in perfection, the first
week in May is generally the best time. But go

there when you will, there is always plenty to
delight anybody, whether he be curious in rare and
beautiful vegetation, or whether he be content to stroll
over sunlit lawns and through shady alleys, with the
shining lakes on either hand, peopled with hundreds
of wild-fowl. The sward is kept to the texture of an
Axminster carpet, with what amount of patient labour
may be guessed from the fact that upwards of seventy
acres are constantly shaven by mowing machines.
It might seem unkind to dwell on these delights if
they were only those of a private pleasure ground ;
but thousands of visitors avail themselves every year
of the considerate decree which opens the gates of
this paradise to the public on two days a week.

In the private flower-garden are some objects of
much interest to botanists and gardeners. The
quaint and beautiful bottle-brush shrub, *Callistemon*,
often erroneously confounded with *Metrosideros* and
usually grown in greenhouses, flourishes on the
terrace near the house with no other protection
than a low wall and a mat cast over it in winter.
It flowers freely and ripens seed every year.
Near to it are such choice things as *Rhaphiolepis
japonica, Clianthus puniceus* and *Eugenia (Myrtus)
apiculata*. In a shrubbery hard by, some of the
more notable plants are various species of *Pittosporum*,
the Nepalese laburnum *(Piptanthus), Acacia dealbata*
twenty feet high,[1] and *Eucalyptus globulus* thirty feet.

[1] Since this was written this plant has succumbed to the frost of 24th April,
1908, which, taking effect upon the vigorous growth induced by preceding heat,
killed it to the ground level.

CASTLE KENNEDY

The last named tree, which stands in a much exposed position, was blown down and killed to the root in the great storm of December, 1894, but has thrown up a new stem.

Taking it all round, Castle Kennedy must be reckoned one of the most remarkable of the larger gardens of Scotland.

THE HIRSEL

" E'S awa to Birgham to buy bickers" is an ancient Border equivoque—how ancient, no man may say. It seems to date from the memorable treaty concluded at Birgham-on-Tweed on 18th July, 1290, defining the relations that should subsist between the realms of England and Scotland after the marriage of the Maid of Norway—Margaret Queen of Scots—to Edward of Carnarvon, Prince of Wales. Death snatched the Maid on her way to the wedding, and there followed three hundred years of "bickers" and butchery between two nations of the same race, speech and creed, the most purposeless and wasteful war that ever drained the resources of a civilised people.

Little enough does Birgham now bear the aspect of a source of strife. Perhaps the old saying was coined in irony because of the inadequacy of this hamlet to sustain a name so great in history, for "bicker" means a wooden bowl as well as a battle. Half a score of grey roofs scattered along a green

84

THE HIRSEL.

ridge are all that mark the birthplace of the War of Independence. Although no part of British soil has been so often soaked with good blood than this vale between Birgham and Coldstream, for the Tweed becomes from Birgham downwards the frontier dividing the two realms, yet nowhere have the traces of conflict been more completely effaced by a veil of verdure and flowers than in Lord Home's pleasant demesne of the Hirsel.

> "Poor heart! above thy field of sorrow sighing
> For broken faith and love untimely slain,
> Leave thou the soil wherein thy dead are lying
> To the soft sunlight and the cleansing rain.
> Love works in silence, hiding all the traces
> Of bitter conflict on the trampled sod,
> And time shall show thee all earth's battle-places
> Veiled by the hand of God."

The very name—The Hirsel—signifying a sheep-fold, breathes pastoral tranquillity, the very antithesis of Lord Home's other residences, to wit—

> "The aventurous castell of Douglass,
> That to kep sa peralous was"—

a place of such wrathful memories that Sir Walter Scott chose it for the scene of his gloomy romance, *Castle Dangerous*; and Bothwell Castle on the Clyde, where the Earls of Hereford and Angus and a few of King Edward's most famous knights sought refuge from the fatal field of Bannockburn, for it was almost the only Scottish fortress where the English flag still flew.

SCOTTISH GARDENS

Outwardly there is nothing in the aspect of the Hirsel to revive memories of the old riding days any more than its present owner, twelfth Earl and seventeenth Lord of Home, could be supposed capable of restoring " Jethart justice," the practice instituted by his ancestor in 1606, when a number of freebooters were first hanged, and then put upon their trial. The mansion is just a country gentleman's roomy residence, built on the banks of the troutful little Leet, and comfortably screened with ample woodland. To view it at its fairest you should go there when May is melting into June, when the trees have just donned their summer finery, and golden broom and fragrant hawthorn turn every country lane into a *chemin de Paradis*.

There is great wealth of rhododendrons in the Hirsel woods, not only the common—far too common— *ponticum*, but the finer hybrid varieties, which are not crowded together in clumps, as one too often sees them arranged, but planted in large measure and with liberal space in the glades of old Scots pine and birch. It is in chequered sunshine and shade that these princely shrubs attain their highest development. Planted in the open, the blossoms get seared by summer heat ; but in thin woodland they display and retain the purest hues.

Eighty years ago Loudon took note of a fine tulip tree growing in the Hirsel garden, reputed at that time to be one hundred years old, and measuring twenty feet in girth at three feet above ground level. The tree

86

is still there, but it is far gone in decay, though it still puts forth plenty of healthy foliage and flowers regularly.

The tulip tree is seldom seen in Scotland; more's the pity, for it is perfectly hardy, its growth is stately and its foliage exquisite. Moreover, the timber is of fine quality, of a clear, light yellow colour, much in request in the United States. Probably the infrequency of its appearance in British woodlands is owing to the difficulty of nursery treatment, owing to the soft and brittle nature of the roots. Also, it requires careful pruning when young to keep it shapely, for it will not stand the removal of large branches in later years. Lastly, the tulip tree must be grown in sheltered spots, for the boughs are very easily broken by high winds.

SOUTH BANTASKINE

STIRLINGSHIRE

HOUGH the plain hums with dirt-producing industry and the west wind darkens the sky with the smoke of a thousand furnaces, yet on clear days the main features of the prospect from the drawing-room windows of South Bantaskine are as grand as they were on that far-off summer day when Wallace's brief, but immortal, career was wrecked by Edward of England (22nd July, 1298), or on that nearer winter day when the star of the Stuarts blazed in dying splendour, and General Hawley's red-coated columns were scattered before the impetuous onset of Lord George Murray's Highlanders (17th January, 1746). For it is here, on the very battle-ground of Falkirk, that the ladies of Bantaskine have furnished their borders with the choicest and brightest blossoms, whereof one of them, Miss Mary Wilson, has prepared the pretty glimpse in Plate XII.

"For life is kind, and sweet things grow unbidden,
　　Turning the field of strife to bloomy bowers;
　Who may declare what secrets may lie hidden
　　Beneath that veil of flowers?"

SOUTH   BANTASKINE.

SOUTH BANTASKINE

Yes, the foreground is greatly altered; and the great central plain of Scotland, which lies around, is tunnelled with mines, punctuated with tall black chimneys and scored with rattling railroads; but beyond all this to the north stand, as of yore, the domes and crests, the cones and cusps, of the Grampians and nearer Ochils.

The spring flush of colour was on the wane and the summer splendour not fully aglow, when I saw this garden; nevertheless, the scene was very fair; for these ladies aim at the fulfilment of Bacon's ideal when he wrote—" I do hold it, in the royal ordering of gardens, there ought to be gardens for all the months of the year; in which, severally, things of beauty may be then in season."

To attain this end the guardians of this place of flowers rely on the commonest material—tulips, hyacinth, narcissus, arabis, myosotis and wallflower in spring—lupins, roses, poppies, pansies and such like in summer. The botanist's borders are apt to appeal only to the elect; where decorative effect is the aim there is nothing to equal the old favourites.

More ambitious, and more laborious to be carried out, is the design which these ladies have undertaken in converting a disused quarry into an alpine garden. It will be a rockwork on a Cyclopean scale. A vast vertical cliff of carboniferous sandstone bounds it on one side, at the foot of which is a fine jumble of fallen boulders and shattered

L   89

shale. No material could be finer for the purpose, but it makes one's back ache to think of the amount of weeding that will be required; for none but those who have put it to the test may realise, not only the incessant diligence which must be exercised to extirpate such vulgar things as pearl-weed, *Marcantia*, sow-thistles, etc., but also the vigilance to prevent *Aubrietia* and *Arenaria* smothering such delicate growths as *Androsace* and *Dianthus*.

I have said that there are not many rare or out-of-the-common plants cultivated at South Bantaskine; one shrub, however, deserves notice as evidence of the climatic capabilities even of this district, which is about the coldest of any at similar elevation in the Scottish Lowlands. *Rhododendron Thomsoni*, one of the most brilliant of a class usually reputed too tender to endure northern winters, has attained a height of eight feet, with a goodly circumference, and looks as if it only required a liberal application of stimulating diet to flower profusely.

COLINTON HOUSE

N almost every instance in Scotland (where such instances are far too frequent), of the abandonment of an ancient fortified dwelling for a mansion in the modern style, one has to deplore the inferiority of the new position to the old. It may have been defensive, rather than æsthetic, features in the ground that guided early architects in their selection of house-sites, but it puzzles one to understand the motive which so often prompted their successors in the nineteenth century to disregard both considerations. In no place that I have visited is the result more to be lamented than at Colinton, once the principal residence of the Foulis family. Perched high upon the steep and wooded east bank of the Water of Leith, the old castle of Colinton, now a roofless ruin, commanded views of exquisite beauty in every direction. The silvan glories of the river valley lay beneath it on the west; on the east the eye might range to the Castle Rock of Edinburgh; while on the south front

91

a terraced garden lies close up to the castle wall, providing a fascinating foreground to the majestic grouping of the Pentland range. A bridle path climbs the shaggy brae from a ford on the river to the castle gate, and an avenue of limes in the bottom rear their lofty tops, yet not so high as to intercept the view from the terrace.

All this rare amenity was sacrificed when, about the end of the eighteenth century, the Colinton estates were broken up and this portion was bought by Sir William Forbes, an Edinburgh banker, who deliberately caused the old castle to be dismantled, and built himself a commodious, but unromantic, mansion a couple of hundred yards away, shutting himself out of sight of the wooded valley, the delectable terrace and garden, and even of the towering Pentland Hills. On the death of Sir William Forbes, Colinton House was purchased by James, third son of General Sir Ralph Abercromby. He was elected Speaker in 1835, and was created Lord Dunfermline in 1839. Dying in 1868, he left Colinton to his only child, the wife of Colonel J. M. Trotter.

The garden remains as of yore, smiling up to the sightless windows of the keep, and lovingly tended by its present owners, Colonel and Mrs. Trotter of Colinton. It has long been noted for the magnificent holly hedges which enclose it, whereof Joseph Sabine, F.R.S., contributed a detailed description to the Horticultural Society of London in 1827

COLINTON HOUSE.

COLINTON HOUSE

(*Transactions,* vol. vii. 194). He stated that these hedges had been planted between 1670 and 1680—"certainly not later than the latter year"; so that at the present time of writing they can be nothing less than 228 years old. At the time of Sabine's visit their height varied from 25 to 28 feet, tapering from a basal diameter of 15 feet to 2 feet at the top. Their present height is from 35 to 40 feet, the basal diameter being in some places as much as 21 feet, the lower branches layering themselves freely and forming an impenetrable rampart. The garden hedges extend in all to a length of 1120 feet, and must have been planted originally with about 4500 hollies. They are clipped at the end of March, which the gardener, Mr. John Bruce, considers the best season, holding that, if the clipping be delayed till July, as most authorities recommend, there is not time for the young growth to ripen before the winter frosts.

Mr. Bruce knows what he is talking about, having had charge of these hedges for thirty-five years; but his employer, Colonel Trotter, takes a different view, believing that June is the best month for pruning evergreens.

The effect of these lofty walls of dark foliage would be somewhat sombre, were the borders not well furnished with bright flowers. In parts of the garden Colonel Trotter relies much for colour on poppies and other annuals, which, at the time Miss Wilson made her study, made but a poor show, owing to the dismal weather of the summer of 1907.

Beside the shrubbery walks outside the garden there are some nice plants of *Berberis Wallichi, Spiræa flagelliformis* and other flowering plants, among which is to be noted an unusually large and symmetrical bush of *Spiræa (Neillea) opulifolia.*

MALLENY

ALLENY was for long in the possession of a family of Scotts—scions of the house of Buccleuch, Laurence Scott being one of the principal Clerks of Session in the reign of James VI. and I. In 1882 it was sold to Lord Rosebery by Lieut.-Col. F. C. Scott, C.B. It is one of those country seats which the growth of Edinburgh has caused to become suburban in its environment, but it remains delightfully secluded, screened by woodland containing some magnificent sycamores. Unluckily I did not visit it until the late tenants, Sir Thomas and Lady Gibson-Carmichael, had resigned their lease from Lord Rosebery, to whom this place belongs, on Sir Thomas being appointed Governor of Victoria. Thus I missed seeing the garden as it should have been seen, for it was Lady Carmichael's care to fill with bright flowers the framework of quaintly clipped yews which are the legacy of bygone generations, while Sir Thomas had enriched all parts of the grounds with weird creatures wrought in metal, in designing and executing which he has earned such a high reputation. Flowers there were still, but not in the luxuriance of former seasons, and the metal work had nearly all been removed. In one respect Malleny is a model for other mansions, especially in Scotland, where modern architects have been allowed too often to banish the flower-garden to an exorbitant distance from the dwelling-house. Here you step from the ivy-grown house direct among the borders, and all the fleeting phases of the season may be enjoyed from the windows. Thus it should ever be in any garden worthy of the name; and thus it seems to have struck Lord Cockburn, who, writing in 1846, mentions Malleny as one of five curious, old-style gardens remaining in Midlothian. "They are all," he said, "sadly injured now. Except Hutton, they were all small and of the same character—evergreen bushes, terraces, and carved stones."

CORROUR

HERE is no more desolate region in all Scotland than that extending northwards from Kinloch-Rannoch to Loch Laggan. Once it was a vast primæval forest broken only by the bare mountain summits, and wherever the surface of the moor is broken, bones of the departed woodland are exposed to view—skeletons of trees lying in inextricable confusion as they fell in a long-forgotten past, embedded in the all-prevailing wet peat. Many theories have been propounded to explain the disappearance of the forest, and the still more obscure cause which prevents trees, when planted now, thriving where millions of them once occupied the ground. The most probable explanation is founded upon a change in meteorological conditions; a cycle of centuries with moderate rainfall, favourable to tree-growth, having been followed by a cycle of centuries with excessive rainfall, encouraging the growth of moss and sphagnum to a degree destructive to higher forms of vegetation, thus causing

M

the total disappearance of forest at about 1000 feet above sea level.

Now as the whole of the district referred to lies above the 1000 feet level, and the only vestiges of the primæval woodland that remain are a few patches of stunted birches and rowans, this might be considered the least likely situation for successful horticulture. So far is this from being the case that, in the very heart of this wilderness, at the unpromising elevation of 1250 feet, there has been created one of the most interesting and effective flower gardens with which I am acquainted. Its prosperity seems to be evidence in support of the theory that it is the excess of rainfall and consequent growth of moss, not low temperature, that destroyed the ancient forest and prevails against all attempts to restore it. Rain falls faster and in greater quantity than evaporation and surface drainage can remove ; the soil becomes water-logged, and moss overwhelms all except such plants as heaths, which are structurally adapted to endure extremes of drought and moisture, heat and cold.

But, it may be argued, the rainfall on the moor ot Rannoch and the surrounding mountains is not greater than in many other districts where trees grow vigorously—the English lake district, for instance. The answer is that altitude must be taken into account. At high levels, cloud prevails much oftener and for longer periods than at lower levels. A few hours of sunshine removes from the earth by evaporation an enormous weight of water, which, under a cloudy sky, can only find escape by gravitation. Consequently, the first requisite in creating a garden in a waterlogged region like Corrour is special provision of rapid drainage. Sir John Stirling Maxwell kept this wisely in view when he chose a site for his shooting lodge at the foot of Loch Ossian. The old lodge, now pulled down, stood 1723 feet above the sea, too high for the growth of the potato, although rhubarb, a true alpine, flourished vigorously in the patch of kitchen garden. The site of the new house is 500 feet lower, built on a terminal moraine, which, by damming back the streams in the strath, has created Loch Ossian, a beautiful sheet of water between three and four miles long. Even at this lower level, corn never ripens, though oats are sown to supply green fodder; whence it may be understood that the creation of a flower garden here was an experiment of no small uncertainty.

Advantage was taken of every natural facility in the ground. The moraine whereon the house stands consists of a vast jumble of granite boulders, ice-borne from the neighbouring mountains. Many of these boulders having crumbled into coarse sand after the peculiar habit of granite, the whole mass was porous, although thickly coated with a mantle of wet peat. That mantle having been got rid of, and a terrace formed along the south front of the house, it was easy to establish a thorough system of drainage, and to maintain it by timely removal of sphagnum. Below this terrace, on the knolls between it and the lake, has been created an alpine garden of the most delightful description.

In alpine gardens and rockeries the effort of make-believe is almost always distressingly obvious. Individual plants may be beautiful and interesting, but the whole effect is unsatisfactory and out of keeping with the environment. But it is otherwise at Corrour. No need to pile rocks in laborious imitation of a ravine; they lie here naturally in profusion as they were thrown down ages ago by the retreating glacier; and as for environment, let the broad flanks and towering crests of Carn Dearg, Beinn Bhreich and Beinn Eibhinn suffice for that, with the fair expanse of Loch Ossian at their feet. To turn this into an alpine garden little more has been necessary than to root out the heather and wild grasses from certain pockets and hollows, fill them with good soil and plant choice bell-flowers, globe flowers, primulas, saxifrages, speedwells, dianthus, and a rich variety of other flowering herbs. It is remarkable to see *Incarvillea Delavayi*, not usually considered patient of excessive wet and cold, flourishing here as luxuriantly as anywhere, spreading into large patches and bearing quantities of its large, gloxinia-like blossoms.

Along the lake margin of yellow sand, iris, spiræa, and other water-loving plants make a charming fringe; while shelter is provided by masses of *Pinus montana*, planted on exposed ridges among the heather. This hardy mountaineer, of dwarf stature but luxuriant foliage, thrives vigorously under

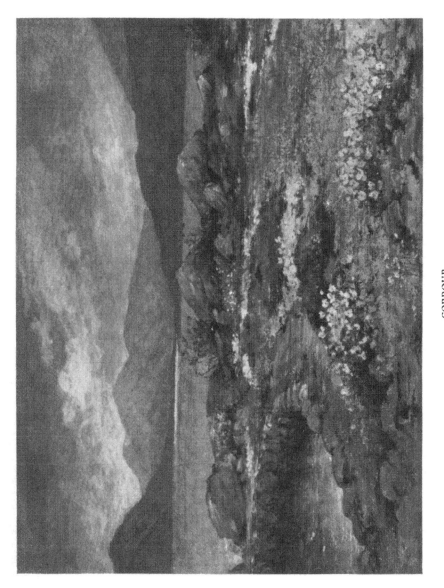

CORROUR.

conditions of exposure and soil which are fatal to other trees. It revels in as much wind as it can get, and is able to digest the humic acid in peat, which is so unfavourable to the health of most trees.

All this part of the ground may be termed wild garden, inasmuch as flowering exotics appear to be growing spontaneously among the native heaths and grasses. But similar effect could not be obtained so easily at a lower altitude than Corrour, where the native herbage has none of the rank exuberance of lowland growth. It is subalpine in character, and is composed of many plants exceedingly ornamental in themselves, such as the various heaths and moorland berries, the field orchises, the dainty little cornel (*Cornus suecica*) and the lovely and fragrant wintergreen (*Pyrola intermedia*). With these are blended in the most natural manner lowly thickets of the Himalayan *Andromeda* (*Cassiope*) *fastigiata*, with terminal racemes of snow-white or flesh-tinted blossoms at the end of every branchlet of intense green. Beside the granite stairs which climb the steeper banks, the great Norwegian saxifrage (*S. cotyledon*) tosses its great cloud of white blossom with a luxuriance that I have never seen equalled elsewhere. The branching sprays and delicate blossoms seem so fragile that one dreads the effect upon them of the first rough breeze; but the stems are so tough and wiry that the display is not marred even by a long Highland gale. Globe-flowers, among which our native *Trollius europæus* holds the palm, crowd the hollow moist places in beautiful contrast with such bell-flowers as *Campanula rhomboidalis.*

The terrace itself, the terrace wall, and the stone borders flanking a granite-margined fountain, are more formal in character. The alpines clothing the wall with a many-coloured mantle seem to display brighter hues than they ever do when cultivated at lower altitudes. Some of them undoubtedly spread more luxuriantly than they do elsewhere. For instance, most gardeners find the Himalayan *Cyananthus lobatus* somewhat difficult to establish—somewhat prone to disappear even when established. Here it may be seen in masses a yard and a half across, covered with shining blue flowers. The matchless turquoise of *Myosotis rupicola* gleams from chinks in the granite stairs in charming contrast with the pearl white of *Oxalis enneaphylla*, the vivid rose of *Dianthus neglectus*, the shining gold of *Waldsteinia trifoliata* and the profound blue of gentianella. This little forget-me-not, not often seen in private gardens, is the choicest of the whole family for wall decoration, for it is compact in habit, growing in dainty tufts, asking only for a narrow, deep crevice, with grit and loam to keep its roots cool, and free space overhead to allow it to enjoy the sunshine.

Notable among scores of pretty herbs on this wall and terrace are wreaths of *Campanula G. F. Wilson*, a hybrid between *C. pulla* and *C. carpatica*, a plant of extraordinary merit owing to the abundance of its dark blue flowers; *Edrianthus* (*Wahlenbergia*) *pumilio*, with a profusion of purple blossom produced from cushions of glaucous, needle-shaped leaves; *Acantholimum glumaceum* spreading into large prickly pillows of green, starred with rosy sprays; the Pyrenean *Globularia nana*; *Oxalis enneaphylla*, a dainty woodsorrel from the Falkland Islands with waxy-white flowers; the beautiful Pyrenean gromwell, *Lithospermum Gastoni*, with sky-blue clusters, and the rare *Gentiana Frœlichi* from Carinthia, with vase-shaped flowers of the same colour.

Spring lags late in these high places; the first snowdrop may not hang its head till its brethren on the seaboard have grown lank and green; but when the frost relaxes its grip and the snow-wreaths sink out of sight, growth comes with a rush, and the profusion of blossom is such as has to be seen before it can be realised.

Gardeners and amateurs owe much to Sir John Stirling Maxwell for having shown by example both at Corrour and Pollok what excellent results may be obtained in decorative horticulture under the most discouraging and apparently prohibitive conditions.

KELLIE CASTLE

NDOUBTEDLY there is more difficulty in fixing upon representative gardens from the east of Scotland than from the west, arising, not from paucity of good subjects, but from their greater frequency. Not that the horticulture of the west is inferior to that of the east; but, as a rule, families resident in the eastern counties have shown more constancy for old walls, and a more conservative sentiment in adapting old houses to modern requirements, than those in the west have done. This was owing partly to the better building material in Lothian, Fife and Aberdeen, and partly to the superior affluence of those districts as compared with the western shires previous to the development of mineral resources. There are notable exceptions, of course, some of which, such as Kelburne and Dalzell, have been assigned a place in this collection; but, on the whole, domestic architecture in the west has suffered far more sweeping changes than it has in the eastward counties.

KELLIE CASTLE.

KELLIE CASTLE

In no place that I have visited does the fleeting present, represented by dainty flowers, appear more closely interwoven with an enduring past, embodied in venerable building, than at Kellie Castle. Standing in the midst of that fertile champaign known as the East Neuk o' Fife, this impressive fortalice—so smiling on its sunward side—so grim and boding on its northern—presents externally much the same aspect as it did before Scotland and England became one realm. Its very environment speaks of a simpler, less affluent age than ours. Here is no far-reaching park, ambitiously planned to yield its lord the impression that the sun and stars circle in the heavens for his sole behoof. Only a narrow belt of aged trees girdles the modest "policies," with cultivated farm-land coming up to the very garden wall, as you may see around many substantial châteaux in France. Nor does the venerable grove contain any of those modern conifers whereof the indiscriminate use has done so much to mar many a pretty pleasure ground. One solitary larch seems almost to apologise for its alien presence among lofty beech and ash trees, massive sycamores, and wych elms.

Before explaining the felicitous circumstance which has preserved the true character of this fine old house, a few notes upon its past may enable the visitor to appreciate the intelligent taste of its present occupants. Originally the principal messuage of the family of Seward or Siward, it passed in 1360 to Sir Walter Oliphant of Gask, who married Elizabeth, natural daughter of Robert the Bruce. The fifth Lord Oliphant, succeeding to the great estates in 1593, so squandered his means by extravagant living that his cousin Patrick, succeeding about 1613, sold the property to Erskine Viscount Fenton, who became Earl of Kellie in 1619. He and his descendants greatly impoverished themselves by their enthusiasm for the Stuart cause, Alexander, the sixth Earl, being among the very few persons of position who went "out" in the '45. An old tree in the garden of Kellie is shown as his temporary hiding place at that time. He paid the penalty of three years' imprisonment, and finally received a free pardon. His son, the seventh Earl, who earned by his musical gifts the sobriquet of "Fiddler Tam," sold his whole estate, except the castle, and two or three hundred acres adjoining, to Sir John Anstruther. In 1875 the fourteenth Earl of Kellie was declared heir to the earldom of Mar in the creation of 1565, and the two earldoms are now united in the person of the twelfth Earl of Mar and fifteenth Earl of Kellie, who rightly sets great store by the beautiful old house which he has inherited, bereft though it be of all but a fragment of the broad lands which once supported it.

By a stroke of rare good fortune, both for the proprietor and all others interested in ancient dwellings, the late Professor James Lorimer took a fancy to the place in 1878. Roofless, floorless, ruinous as was the castle, he obtained a long lease of it and proceeded to reconstruct the fallen work, repair the rest, and re-create the whole grounds and garden in the spirit of the seventeenth century. Admirably did he succeed, and, although he has passed away, his widow and his son, Mr. R. S. Lorimer, A.R.S.A., most faithfully and tenderly carry on his plan and purpose, which is explained and commemorated by an inscription graven over the entrance:

HOC · DOMICILIVM · CORVIS · ET · BVBONIBVS · EREPTVM
HONESTO · INTER · LABORES · OTIO · CONSECRATVM · EST
A·S·   J·A·H·L
MDCCCLXXVIII[1]

"To me, as an architect," writes Mr. R. S. Lorimer, "the interesting point about the house is that the plan has not been interfered with or modernised, and the exterior of the house is practically untouched. So many of the fine old Scotch houses were ruined by Bryce and others fifty or sixty years ago, the old portion being entirely surrounded by modern work; whereas, when it is necessary to add to an old Scotch house, the old portion ought to be allowed to stand up and tell its own story, and the new portion should be joined on to it by some narrow neck so that there never can be any question as to which is the old and which is the new.

"One of the characteristics of Kellie is the fact that the walled garden enters direct out of the house, and that the flowers, and fruit, and vegetables are all mixed up together.

"I always think the ideal plan is to have the park, with the sheep or beasts grazing in it, coming right under the windows at one side of the house, and the gardens attached

---

[1] "This dwelling, having been cleared of crows and owls, has been devoted to honourable repose from labour." The legend was written by the late Principal Sir Alexander Grant.

to the house at another side. We could not quite manage this at Kellie but put as light a fence as possible between the lawn and the park."

The castle garth, with its sunny grey walls, archway of clipped yew, trellised roses, and thick box edging a couple of feet high, has been kept much as it must have been when "Fiddler Tam" made it resound with the strains of his violin. The charm of eld, so difficult of attainment by any accelerating process, hallows every bush and border. Little is grown here except the common old favourites of our great-grandmothers ; some fine plants of *Piptanthus nepalensis*, flowering luxuriantly at the time of my visit, seemed scarcely at home among their eighteenth century neighbours. A modern garden house, with stone roof and shadowy eaves, at the north-east corner of the garth, has been so deftly brought into harmony with a distant past, as to cheat one into believing it to be part of the original design.

And over all this tranquil scene presides the time-worn fortalice, with its crow-stepped gables and clustered *tourelles*, prompting the inevitable, invariable wish—"Ah, could these walks but speak!" "Futile!" say you. Nay, but they do speak, and have much to tell to understanding hearers.

> "All pain, all passion, all regret,
> All love and longing come
> To swell the strain whose burden yet
> Imploreth 'Home, sweet home.'"

AUCHENCRUIVE

O one can realise, until he tries it, the difficulty of making a small selection from the many beautiful gardens to be found in every Scottish county. There are famous gardens, such as those at Dalkeith, Drumlanrig, Preston Hall, Drummond Castle, Terregles, and many other places, to which we would fain have given a place in these pages, had they not been described and depicted in so many previous publications. Our purpose has been, not to present the well-known and distinguished, but rather to point out in how many gardens, humble as well as lordly, beauty is to be found by anybody who cares to look for it.

Many charming homes have been built and many delightful pleasure grounds laid out in the immediate neighbourhood of

> "Auld Ayr, wham ne'er a town surpasses
> For honest men and bonny lasses,"

but there is no garden in that district to be compared with that of Auchencruive for natural charm of rock and river, sequestered glades and shaggy cliffs. There are gardens elsewhere more noteworthy than this one for their contents—for extensive collections of exotics or remarkable specimens of individual species. It cannot be denied that the owners of Auchencruive, past and present, have displayed little ambition in these respects, and this the enthusiast may feel inclined to regret, for undoubtedly there are the means here, on a friable soil in a western climate, with abundant shelter from violent winds, of cultivating the choicer kinds of trees and shrubs mentioned in Appendices A and B.

Nevertheless, natural features have not been neglected; breadth of effect has been well secured by contrast of massive woodland with liberal spaces of turf; brightness has been obtained by beds of roses and the ordinary border flowers; and through this fair scene flows the river Ayr, here churning into foam among reefs of red sandstone, there sweeping in glassy reaches under the shade of venerable trees.

Miss Wilson has chosen for her subject the cliff which falls sheer from the bluff whereon the mansion-house is built, and which has been skilfully wrought into a hanging garden in a series of galleries rather than terraces. It is a notable feature, and confers an air of distinction upon what might otherwise be remembered as merely a very pretty garden. Sameness is not so prevalent a vice in decorative horticulture as it was five-and-twenty years ago. It is the

AUCHENCRUIVE.

exception now to meet with a lady presiding over a country house who feels indifferent to the contents of her flower-beds. Most ladies, and many men, now take an active interest in cultivating a variety of flowering things. Disraeli had a hand in turning the attention of people of leisure to this source of enjoyment and perennial occupation. Probably no subject of Queen Victoria was more ignorant of the processes of horticulture. Had he been asked the definition of a herbaceous plant he would have found refuge in an epigram. But he had the saving grace of imagination which enabled him to perceive that beds of "Mrs. Pollock" geranium and "Countess of Stair" ageratum were no more capable than a Brussels carpet of inspiring affection. *Pereunt et non imputantur.* They carry with them no associations—are redolent with no tender memories. Therefore, desiring to depict Corisande as devoted to her flowers, Disraeli filled her garden with old-world perennials—plants more abiding than the generations of men, yielding blossoms year by year to the children's children of those who set them in the borders. And, when Disraeli had stirred people's fancy with a longing for the old flowers that they could love, Mr. William Robinson began to teach them how that longing might be realised, and he has lived to see the revolution complete.

There is an end to sameness in gardens, but the risk of tameness is as great as ever. A dominant

111

feature, like the flowery cliff at Auchencruive, preserves a garden from the one defect as much as from the other. I remember the Auchencruive garden thirty years ago when sameness and tameness were at their height, and that cliff stands out in memory, wreathed with bright flowers, the broad river at its foot sparkling in the sunlight and glimmering in green gloom of old oaks on the further shore.

At Auchencruive one is in the very heart of what railway companies and hotel managers never weary of proclaiming as the Land of Burns. Very characteristic of the *vates sacer*, though hardly creditable to his sense of delicacy, are the verses in which two successive mistresses of the house of Auchencruive are commemorated. The first of these was wife of that Richard Oswald whom Shelburne appointed in 1782 as Minister-Plenipotentiary to negotiate the treaty with the United States. Burns never met her living, but in January, 1789, when riding through Nithsdale, he stopped for the night at Sanquhar.

"The frost was keen," he wrote to Dr. Moore, "and the grim evening and howling wind were ushering in a night of snow and drift. My horse and I were both much fatigued with the labours of the day; and just as my friend the bailie [Whigham] and I were bidding defiance to the storm over a smoking bowl, in wheels the funeral pageantry of the late Mrs Oswald; and poor I am forced to brave all the terrors of the tempestuous night, and jade my horse—my young favourite horse whom I had just christened Pegasus—further on, through the wildest hills and moors of Ayrshire, to New Cumnock, the next inn! The powers of poesy and prose sink under me when I would describe what I felt. Suffice it to say that, when a good fire at New Cumnock had so far recovered my frozen sinews, I sat down and wrote the enclosed ode."

Dr. Moore had done well for his friend if he had suppressed the said ode, for slander grosser and more gratuitous was never penned than this lampoon upon a lady, who, during her life, had never given the writer cause of offence. Nevertheless, his case was a hard one; he did but express in stinging verse the irritation which one of us lesser mortals would have vented in bad language.

The other composition was of a very different character, and, in its later form, celebrated the charms of the wife of the first lady's grandson, M.P. for Ayrshire. Her name was Louisa, which, for the sake of metre, was altered to Lucy in the poem. The husband is supposed to be singing the praises of his wife.

> " O, wat ye wha's in yon town,
>   Ye see the e'enin' sun upon ?
> The fairest dame's in yon town
>   That e'enin' sun is shining on."

Such is the refrain of eight fervent stanzas; but woe's me for Robin's constancy! The verses were originally addressed to Jean Armour—the "bonnie Jean" of many an ode. To adapt them to another fair one's acceptance, "maid" had to be altered to "dame," and "Jeannie" to "Lucy!" Conscientious editors have duly chronicled in footnotes the variant readings.

BARSKIMMING

T is a fancy of certain writers to give freak headings to their chapters, cryptic enough, sometimes, but connected more or less vaguely with the nature of the contents. Were that example to be followed in the present unimaginative work, this chapter might be entitled "Cheese and Chaffinches," to commemorate a pretty little scene enacted in that fairyland which mortals call Barskimming.

The river Ayr winds through the park, having cut for itself a profound channel through the red Permian rock which overlies the carboniferous beds in all this part of Ayrshire. The sides of the gorge are richly clothed with oak and ash, which, as appears from Timothy Pont's survey, executed in 1595-1600, are survivors of the primitive Caledonian forest; but here and there the sides are sheer precipice, affording no foothold for trees, the crags standing out bare, silvered with lichen or glowing with venetian red and rose where the rock has crumbled away. In front of the mansion

114

BARSKIMMING.

house, which was rebuilt after a fire some five-and-twenty years ago, a lofty and beautiful bridge, designed by Robert Adam, has been flung across the chasm.

Of the four sisters who have made Barskimming their home for a number of years, each has her peculiar province and chosen outlet for energy. Miss Marianne Anderson has established and made famous a stud of Welsh mountain ponies, a breed whereof she was among the first to recognise the extraordinary beauty and quality, and which has secured for her many honours at Dublin and other horse shows. Miss Fanny Anderson's specialty is ornamental ironwork, the garden gate, through which we shall pass presently, being an example of the combined strength and delicacy of her handiwork. She has also a remarkable power of attraction for wild birds. Whether this be psychical, or whether it be purely physical, residing in a small tin box stuck in her waist-belt, deponent sayeth not ; he can but testify to what he saw. Pausing on the bridge aforesaid on our way to the garden, the bird-compeller sounded shrill summons to her familiars, and forthwith there came from the dense foliage of an aged oak, whose topmost branches were several feet below the bridge, a hen chaffinch, to perch on the parapet within a yard or two of where we leant. A second hen followed, and after her a cock bird, not quite so confident. Then the magic box was opened, disclosing some tiny bits of cheese. One of the birds was so tame as to take a piece of this delicacy from the very lips of the lady ; but the favourite exhibition is obtained by flicking a morsel of cheese over the parapet, when the chaffinches dart in pursuit, one or other of them never failing to catch it before it reaches the water eighty feet below.

But our main business at Barskimming lies to-day in the garden, where Miss Bertha Anderson reigns supreme, and thither she now guides us, through the pretty gate mentioned above. Miss Bertha's collection of flowering plants has gained wide repute, but before examining it in detail, a few words must be devoted to describing the pleasaunce wherein they flourish, for it is quite distinct in character from any other depicted in this book. Through the heart of it the Powkail[1] has cleft a deep cañon in its haste to join the river which bounds the garden on the south. With dubious taste, Lord Glenlee, the Scottish Lord of Session who laid out these grounds 140 years ago, caused this stream to run for some distance through a tunnel, filling up the dark gorge and levelling the surface as a bowling green. The lower part of its course, which remains open, shows how much natural beauty was sacrificed in this costly operation. However, there it is ; a fair space of level turf, partly shaded from the south by splendid oaks

[1] Celtic names cling closely to the topography of the Lowlands. Powkail—the narrow stream—from the Gaelic *pol caol*, containing the same word as has been used for centuries to denote the Kyles—that is the Narrows—of Bute.

of the true sessile-flowered kind, and bounded on the other sides by sloping banks, terraced walks, and flower borders. The north and west sides of the garden are protected by old and high walls, once occupied by fruit-trees and a grape-house, but these Miss Bertha has swept into limbo, draping the walls instead with sheets of climbers, especially roses, among which may be noted the snowy Mme. Alfred Carrière (well shown in Miss Wilson's drawing), the long streamers of the original Loudon rose, putative parent of the numerous progeny known as Ayrshire roses, and the Letton briar, a very uncommon variety, with large, single flowers of clear, full pink.

Having got so far, the visitor will have begun to realise some of the features which give its distinguished character to this little valley of flowers. Chief, perhaps, among these is the combination of a very dry surface with the perennial presence of swiftly running water. No Eden is perfect without its stream, and here gushing Powkail sounds ever in one's ears as it hurries to the river through a deep and narrow dell, planted with choice ferns and shade-loving plants. The Canadian *Adiantum pedatum* luxuriates here; *Primula rosea* attains a stature impossible under ordinary conditions; the pretty foam flower (*Tiarella cordifolia*) runs riot among the moist rocks, the yellow and orange forms of the Welsh poppy mingle in charming contrast with the clear blue of *Campanula rhomboidalis. Rodgersias* spread their noble foliage, meet companions for the native wood bell-flower (*C. latifolia*) and the giant saxifrage (*S. peltata*). It is a place to make patent the futility and self-consciousness of so many rock gardens; it is indeed inimitable by most gardeners, for the foot of man can never have passed through this gorge until Miss Bertha caused paths to be hewn out of the vertical rocks and flung a bridge here and there across the chasm.

The license of flower and foliage which riots in this dell throws into high relief the perfect order and neatness maintained in the rest of the grounds. Neatness without formality. There is not a gravel or paved path in the whole garden; nothing but shaven sward on which you walk as upon velvet pile—sward in green lagoons, as it were, across which splendid oaks fling broad shadows—sward in smooth alleys between banks of summer flowers which have succeeded the spring bulbs, now fast asleep in the mould—sward in bays and corridors among choice rhododendrons and a few, not too many, conifers. Here and there, in sunny nooks, stand pillars of a peculiar kind, supporting large pots of geraniums. These pillars come from neighbouring Mauchline, famous for its curling stones, and are the sandstone rollers upon which the harder curling stones have been ground. The sandstone wears away in grooves and rolls, causing the core to assume an architectural character, in which Miss Bertha's quick eye detected decorative properties. Two of these rollers, set one upon another, make a pillar about five feet high, and, being waste products, can be had for little more than the cost of carriage.

Now as to the flower borders, with their varied contents and their fine combination of freedom with discipline, one has to remember that every plant has to withstand the climate of a cold Ayrshire upland about 400 feet above the sea. This, therefore, is not one of those gardens whereof the owner is lured to disappointment by attempting the open-air culture of plants just outside the limits of perfect hardiness. Miss Bertha contents herself with things which will flourish anywhere in the British Isles, provided that they are wisely handled. The greater the surprise, therefore, to find a bed of Ixias in luxuriant blossom. The bulbs were planted at the beginning of January, 1907, and, in virtue of a perfectly drained and light soil, withstood the rigours of twenty-five degrees of frost and a peculiarly trying spring. We do not, however, recommend an attempt to grow these gay flowers in the north, except for a single season's display. Like the Persian ranunculus, they require baking in hotter sunshine than our Scottish firmament permits, to prepare them for a second year's display of their brilliant colours.

The general effect of the borders at the time of our visit was given by larkspurs, roses, iris and campanula of many kinds, the most distinct of the bell-flowers being the rich blue species now classed as *C. rhomboidalis*, though why in the world it

119

should be deprived of its former and most appropriate epithet *azurea* is one of those mysteries wrought in the star chamber of Kew. Among these were several choice flowers not often met with, such as *Oxalis Deppii*, a woodsorrel with flowers, large for this genus, of *vieux rose*, greatly superior to the commoner *O. floribunda*. *Lathyrus Drummondi* (*rotundifolius*), with blossoms of fine cinnabar red, rambled over aged espalier apple-trees in the back row; *Salvia tenori* was conspicuous afar with its deep blue spikes, and *Veronica pimeloides* poured a little cataract of greyish-blue from the front row.

The nucleus, so to speak, of this paradise of flowers, is a rectangular kitchen garden in the old style, with narrow borders along the paths, backed by espalier fruit trees screening off the cabbages and onions. But so deftly has this part of the ground been handled, so generously have the flowering plants responded to liberal and discriminate treatment, that one does not suspect the presence of *utile* among such a wealth of *dulce*. There it is, however, though it requires close scrutiny to detect it, and I do not remember to have seen elsewhere this combination of flower and kitchen garden so skilfully carried out. Weeds, it may be assumed, are as aggressive at Barskimming as elsewhere, but the hand of the Mistress of the Flowers is as ready as her eye is quick: not a nettle nor bit of groundsel is to be found in all the borders over which she holds sway, so vigilantly does she carry out the first principles of horticulture—selection and rejection.

I cannot leave Barskimming without mentioning one picturesque, if homely, feature in its garden. Every amateur and professional gardener must have realised the difficulty of disposing of rubbish. In the outskirts of nearly every pleasure-ground there exists a dire accumulation, more or less successfully concealed, of rotting cabbage stalks, flower stems, decayed fruit, old pease-sticks, etc., mounting higher year by year, abode of rats, and source of evil odours. Scottish gardeners speak of this as "the coup"; I know not what the southron synonym may be. Well, at Barskimming "the coup" is on a heroic scale. All the waste products, which will not serve for leaf-mould, are shot over a sheer precipice on the south side of the garden, and fall clear nearly 100 feet into the river Ayr, to be swept away by the first spate.

And spates are neither niggardly nor infrequent in Western Scotland.

CAWDOR CASTLE

ARIOUS are the elements which go to make a perfect garden, each of them appealing in its degree to different persons according to their temperament and training. Not very numerous are those competent to criticise the technicalities of cultivation, but the pleasure is very complete which their knowledge enables them to derive from a visit to a collection so large and intelligently tended as Mr. William Robinson's at Gravetye Manor or Canon Ellacombe's well-stored grounds at Bitton Vicarage. Historic association or romantic tradition appeals to a larger number, and these will be as agreeably moved by gazing on the bleak formality of Diane de Poictiers' garden at Chenonceaux as by the enchanting groves into which they pass through Ibn-l-Ahmar's Gate of Pomegranates in the Alhambra.

For such persons the ample grace of the gardens at Hatfield will be enhanced by their antiquity, and the recollection that the pleached lime-trees and venerable mulberries were planted for the delectation of Robert

122

CAWDOR CASTLE.

CAWDOR CASTLE

Cecil, first Earl of Salisbury, when he became the reluctant owner of that manor, having been compelled by King James to receive it in exchange for beloved Theobalds in 1607.

Perhaps a majority of practical people agree with Mr. Andrew Lang's opinion that "gardens were devised by Providence for the pottering peace of virtuous eld," and are satisfied with a garden if it soothes their senses by a tasteful disposition of trees, and shrubs, and flowering herbs. The nearest approach to perfection is attained in a garden where the eye is gratified by beauty of form and colour, and the mind is stimulated by historic association; and such is the case at Cawdor Castle. It is as impossible, one would think, to visit this seat of the ancient Thanes and remain indifferent to the strange narrative which men claim to be its history, as it would be to derive no pleasure from the contrast of masses of bright blossom with the grim grey towers which overlook them.

Cawdor Castle stands in the midst of that rich strath which stretches from the foot of Carn-nan-tri-tighearnan, or the Cairn of the Three Lords, to the sea. On the east, dark Findhorn battles his way to the Moray Firth through the gorges of Altyre and Relugas; on the west, the little Nairn prattles and sparkles along its pebbly channel, parallel to the greater river. We are fully four hundred miles north of Greenwich here, yet the climate of this region, summer and winter, is perhaps the most delightful of any part of the British Isles. No wonder that possession of this choice territory was fiercely contested in days when the sword was stronger than the pen.

The Thanes of Cawdor claimed descent from that brother to whom Macbeth, Mormaer of Moray, yielded the thanedom when he usurped the throne of Scotland in 1040 ; but it was not until 1454 that the family rose to be important in the person of Thane William, who was appointed by James II. to administer the broad lands of Moray, forfeited to the Crown on the fall of the great house of Douglas in that year.

Thane William's castle at that time was at Invernarne, now called Nairn ; but he had also a hunting lodge some six miles inland at Old Cawdor. The narrow tower of Nairn appearing inadequate for his new and lucrative dignity, he determined to build a larger stronghold. More prudent than the generality of Scottish lairds, he laid by the necessary cash in a strong box before a single stone was laid, deliberating the while on the choice of a suitable site. The problem, it may be supposed, occupied much of his thoughts, waking and sleeping. One night a brilliant suggestion came to him in a dream, which bade him bind the treasure on the back of an ass, turn the beast loose at Old Cawdor, and found his castle wherever it should first lie down. In the age of faith, nothing could be more natural than that the Thane should fulfil literally the instructions received in a dream, and this he did to the letter.

124

CAWDOR CASTLE

Now the ass, being heavily laden with cash, which tradition reports was contained in an iron chest, did not wander far. It browsed its way slowly to a knoll below the confluence of Allt Dearg and the Rierach Burn, whereon grew three hawthorns, under one of which it lay down. The castle keep was built round the tree, which sceptics may handle and see at this day, dry and sapless it is true, but still hard and sound, rooted in the floor and built into the vaulted roof of the donjon. Beside it lies the iron coffer which once held the treasure, and from time to time guests in the castle gather round these venerable relics and quaff—"Success to the hawthorn tree," though it has borne neither leaves nor flowers these four hundred and fifty years.

This keep is but the core of the vast pile which now frowns down upon the beautiful garden represented in Miss Wilson's painting. The greater part of the castle as it stands was the work of Colin Campbell in 1639. How the Campbells came to Cawdor is explained in several versions of a tradition, differing in detail, but agreeing in the main facts. Here, briefly, is one account of the transaction thoroughly in keeping with the times.

Thane William, builder of the keep, was succeeded by his son William, who had five sons, all of whom were childless, except John, who married Isobel Rose of Kilravock. John died in 1498, shortly after the birth of his only child, Muriel, who, succeeding to the thanedom and its ample revenues, instantly became an object of supreme interest to other powerful landowners. Among these was Archibald, second Earl of Argyll, who was particularly anxious to find suitable matches for his younger sons. Being Lord High Chancellor of Scotland and a prime favourite with James IV., Argyll obtained from that monarch the ward of Muriel's marriage. But the child's three uncles were not disposed to admit Muriel's succession, which they claimed as limited to heirs male. They refused, therefore, to surrender the babe to Argyll, who straightway adopted means to enforce his rights in the old manner. He sent his vassal Campbell of Innerliver,[1] with sixty clansmen, to capture his ward. Concealing themselves in the wood of Cawdor, they waited till the nurse brought out baby Muriel, scarcely more than a year old, for an airing near the castle. The ambush was a success ; the child was easily taken, but not before the nurse, with a wholesome suspicion of Highland ways, had bitten off a joint from the little finger of her charge, in order to her better identification in future possible contingencies.

The Campbells struck out for distant Lochowe with their precious little prisoner; but the nurse ran back to rouse the castle. The uncles set forth hot-foot in pursuit of the kidnappers, overtook and attacked them with a superior force. Inverliver, seeing his men overpowered, shouted—"'*S fhada*

[1] Innerliver or Inverliever was purchased in 1907 by the Commissioners of Woods and Forests in order to form a State forest. It extends to about 13,000 acres.

glaodh o' Lochow! '*S fhada cobhair o chlann dhoaine!*"
That is, "It's a far cry to Lochowe! and succour is
far from my lads in their danger!" Then he had
recourse to an ingenious ruse. Having caused the
baby to be stripped and her clothes stuffed with
straw, he thrust the bundle under a large camp
kettle inverted, taking care that the enemy should
have full view of the latter part of the proceeding.
Then he set his seven sons round the kettle, charg-
ing them to defend it to the death, and, drawing
off the survivors of his band, escaped with them
and the babe into the wilds of Monadh Lia.

The seven young men all perished at their
appointed post ; but when the bereaved uncles raised
the kettle—lo! there was nothing but a bundle of
straw and some baby's clothing.

When Muriel was brought to Lochowe, the nurse's
sagacity in mutilating her was justified.

· "What shall we do," asked Campbell of Auchin-
leck, "if she dies before she is of marriageable age?"

"She can never die," answered Inverliver, "so
long as a red-haired lassie can be found on the
shores of Lochowe!"

Muriel remained in custody of the Campbells
till the year 1510, when, being twelve years of age,
she was duly married to John, third son of the
Earl of Argyll, from which union the present Earl
Cawdor is tenth in direct male descent : and that is
how the Campbells came to Cawdor.

Other and later memories people the landscape

that rolls, ridge upon ridge, away to the bleak expanse of Monadh Lia. Every glen cherishes its tradition of the terrible spring of 1746, when, after the sun of the Stuarts had set for ever in blood and tears on the fatal moor of Culloden, Cumberland's troops were dispersed in pursuit of the broken clans. Scores of stout fellows, many of them grievously wounded, were hunted down like hill-foxes and butchered in cold blood. Their children's children will still point out to you the very spots where the horrid work went on, so grievously was Lord President Forbes mistaken when he wrote to Walpole—"If all the rebels, with their wives, children, and dependants, could be rooted out of the earth, the shock would be astonishing, *but time would commit it to oblivion.*"

It were well, perhaps, could that month's work be blotted from the records of the British army; but let us not forget another deed of blood committed in this district about the same time. Two or three miles west of Lord Cawdor's shooting lodge of Drynachan is the place of Pall-a-chrocain, whereof the laird MacQueen died in 1797. He was of gigantic stature, six foot seven inches, they say, in Highland brogues (which have no heels), and a mighty hunter before the Lord. In the winter of 1743-4 a woman was crossing the hill between Cawdor and the Findhorn with her two children, when she was set upon by a large wolf, which carried one of them away. The alarm was sounded; the laird of

MacIntosh summoned a "tainchel" or great hunting to assemble at Fi-Giuthas, not far from Pall-a-chrocain. MacQueen, of course, was invited; indeed, no such hunting could be reckoned complete without that individual and his famous dogs. But on the appointed morning the laird of Pall-a-chrocain failed to appear at the right time. The party waited—the MacIntosh swore—the early morning was the only time when there was a chance of picking up the trail of the nocturnal marauder. At last, Pall-a-chrocain was seen striding across the heather towards them at a leisurely pace. MacIntosh addressed him pretty sharply, complaining that he had kept them all waiting.

"Ciod e a' chabhag? (What's the hurry)," said Pall-a-chrocain, coolly; whereat the impatient hunters gave an angry growl and the chief waxed still more indignant.

"Sin e dhuib! (There it is then!)," said the delinquent, and, throwing back his plaid, flung down the wolf's head at their feet. He had stolen a march upon his friends; but it seems that they were bent on business, rather than sport, for it is recorded that they were all delighted, and that the MacIntosh rewarded Pall-a-chrocain by giving him the land of Seanachan "for meat to his dogs."

This appears really to have been the last wolf killed in all Scotland, for, although Pennant assigned to Sir Ewen Cameron the honour of having put an end to the race in 1680, the animal slain on that occasion was only the last in Lochaber.

MANSE OF FYVIE

HE Ythan, beloved of trout-fishers, flows through a fair strath enriched with many memories and set with many an ancient fortalice. Transcending all others in Aberdeenshire—perhaps in all Scotland—for architectural interest is the magnificent castle of Fyvie, whereof the history has its source in days long before Edward I. of England made it his lodging in 1296, and bids fair to outlast by many centuries the visit of Edward VII. of Great Britain and Ireland (and a good deal else besides) in 1907. When the annals of a house extend over so many centuries, trifling chronological inexactitudes may be treated with leniency; still, it taxes our credulity rather beyond its limits to be shown in the fifteenth century Seton tower at Fyvie the actual bedroom occupied by the first Edward in the thirteenth century! In truth, there is no part of the building which can be declared confidently to have belonged to the original stronghold, so completely has the whole castle undergone reconstruction by successive

MANSE OF FYVIE.

owners. Nevertheless it remains almost without a rival as an example of the peculiar Scottish style.

So sweetly the woods and fields smile under the fleecy clouds, so blue are the hill-crests and so sparkling the streams, that we cannot grudge the hours as the leisurely "local" wends its way from Aberdeen on this perfect summer day. In due time we alight (in literature people do not "get out" of trains and carriages, they "alight") on the platform of Fyvie station. There is a choice of ways thence to our destination—the legitimate one by the high road, but that has been robbed of much of its charm by the interminable park wall which Lord Leith of Fyvie recently caused to be built for the relief of the unemployed ; so we take the other, illegitimate perhaps, to mere wayfarers as we are, but Scottish landowners are never illiberal in the matter of trespass. Entering the "policies" of Fyvie at the lodge gate, a delightful woodland walk leads across the little river, under the walls of the castle and out along the margin of a lake till we reach the open country again.

Below us on the right is the bridge of Sleugh where Annie of Tifty Mill[1] parted for ever with her lover—a tragedy commemorated in a ballad which became dearer, perhaps, than any other to Aberdeenshire people. It tells how pretty Agnes, daughter

[1] Her baptismal name was Agnes, but she always appears as Nannie or Annie in the various versions of the ballad.

of the wealthy miller of Tifty, lost her heart to a handsome trumpeter in the suite of the Lord of Fyvie.

> "At Fyvie's yett there grows a flower,
>   It grows baith braid and bonnie;
> There's a daisy in the midst o' it,
>   And they call it Andrew Lammie."

No backward lover was the said daisy, for the maiden tells us how—

> "The first time me and my love met
>   Was in the woods o' Fyvie,
> He kissed my lips five thousand times
>   And aye he ca'd me bonnie."

The miller, whose name does not appear in the poem, but who is known to have borne the homely one of Smith, took a very firm line with his daughter from the first. He declined even to entertain the idea of her wedding with a mere trumpeter. She should look far higher for a mate with her "tocher" of five thousand merks. The miller's wife and sons were of the same opinion, and between them they led poor Annie a terrible life. If the poet is to be credited, when argument failed, they tried violence and beat the girl unmercifully. They even showed Lord Fyvie the door when he came to plead the cause of the lovers. Annie remained true to her troth, and before Andrew's duty called him away to Edinburgh he met her in a last tryst at the Bridge of Sleugh, and vowed he would come back and marry her in spite of them all.

MANSE OF FYVIE

Now there is an old Scottish belief that lovers who part at a bridge will meet never more ; and so it proved with this fond couple. Annie died, some say of a broken heart, others of a broken back owing to her brother's brutality.

> " When Andrew hame frae Embro' cam
> Wi' muckle grief and sorrow—
> ' My love is dead for me to-day,
> I'll die for her to-morrow.
>
> " ' Now will I speed to the green kirkyard,
> To the green kirkyard o' Fyvie ;
> With tears I'll water my love's grave,
> Till I follow Tifty's Annie.' "

No doubt was ever cast on Andrew's fidelity ; but although he may have mourned over his sweetheart's grave, he did not stay in the kirkyard, for it is told of him that long after her death he was in a company in Edinburgh where the ballad of *Tifty's Annie* was sung, which so deeply affected him that the buttons flew off his doublet ! A stone in " the green kirkyard of Fyvie " bears the following inscription :

HEIR · LYES · AGN
ES · SMITH · WHO
DEPARTIT · THE
19 · OF · JANVARI
1673.

while Andrew Lammie is commemorated by a stone figure of a trumpeter on the battlements of one of the castle towers.

SCOTTISH GARDENS

But our errand to-day is not to gather up on the spot the threads of this sad story, nor to view the lordly castle, nor yet to explore the foundations of S. Mary's Priory, built by Fergus Earl of Buchan in 1179 for the Tironensian monks of S. Benedict, or to deplore the completeness of its demolition. There stands the castle, but there does *not* stand the priory, though its site is well marked by a tall Celtic cross, set up in 1868 on a green knoll, and far seen up and down the strath. The object of our mission lies close to "the green kirkyard of Fyvie," whither Miss Wilson's instinct for fair flowers directed her, with the result shown in Plate XIX.

A keen instinct it is shown to be, for it is a melancholy but general truth that the manse garden is about the last place in a Scottish parish that one expects to find well-tended borders. In England it is different ; it is among the English clergy that you may look for some of the most accomplished amateurs, and, as high authorities in horticulture, it would be hard to beat Dean Hole for roses, Mr. Engleheart for daffodils, or Canon Ellacombe for all sorts of flowering things. The Scottish clergy, as a class, are strangely indifferent to the fluctuating hopes and fears, joys and woes, of horticulture. There are notable and praiseworthy exceptions, but I speak of the class, with the necessary *caveat* about generalising. I scarcely think that our pastors of to-day can be deterred from seeking solace in an occupation so natural and congenial to men whose avocation keeps

134

them in country homes throughout most of the months, or that they have any such apprehension of censure as induced good Dr. Nathaniel Paterson seventy years ago to withhold his name from the title-page of the first edition of his delightful *Manse Garden*.

"The following work," he explained in the introduction, "though nowise contrary to clerical duty, is nevertheless not strictly clerical; and as nothing can equal the obligation of the Christian ministry, or the awe of its responsibility, or its importance to man, the writer trembles at the thought of lessening, by any means or in any degree, either the dignity or the sacredness of his calling; and as the following pages might more properly have been written by one bred to the science of which they treat, or by some leisurely owner of a retired villa, an inference, not the best matured, may be drawn to the effect—that surely the Author can be no faithful labourer in the Lord's Vineyard, seeing he must possess such a leaning to his own. He therefore expects, by hiding for a little, to give the arrow less nerve, because the bowman can only shoot into the air, not knowing whither to direct his aim."

It may be deemed presumptuous for a layman to criticise the recreations of his spiritual masters. Assuredly I do so in no carping spirit, but out of sheer concern for the neglect of so harmless and convenient a hobby. For is not every man happier with a hobby? And in riding this particular hobby gently, a country clergyman may lead the way for his parishioners to do the like. Hear what comfortable words the aforesaid Dr. Paterson spoke upon this matter.

"When home is rendered more attractive, the market-gill will be forsaken for charms more enduring, as they are also more endearing and better for both soul and body. And O! what profusion of roses and ripe fruits, dry gravel and shining laurels, might be had for a thousandth part of the price given for drams . . . Thus external things, in themselves so trivial as the planting of shrubs, are great when viewed in connection with the moral feelings whence they proceed and the salutary effects which they produce. . . Wherever such fancy for laudable ornament is found (and it is a thing which, like fashion, spreads fast and far), the pastor, by suggesting this guide to simple gardening, may do a kindness to his flock."

Now let me descend from the pulpit which I have usurped, and enter the manse garden which I have brought the reader so far to see. Favoured by fortune as few gardens of this class have been, it has passed successively through hands which have carefully tended it. Various stories are told to account for the amplitude of the kitchen garden and the high walls enclosing it. According to one version, these walls were the gift of his wife to a former incumbent, Mr. Manson, and, scarcely was the mortar dry in them when the Disruption of the Kirk came to pass (in 1843), and Mr. Manson "went out," surrendering his benefice and forsaking his beloved garden—for conscience' sake. Another variant attributes these walls to another lady, wife of the Rev. John Falconer, who was minister from 1794 to 1828, immediate predecessor of the aforesaid Mr. Manson. After Mr. Manson's resignation, Dr. Cruikshank was translated from Turriff to Fyvie, and married Mr. Falconer's widow, thus inheriting the walls.[1] Dr. Milne followed Dr. Cruikshank in 1870, and there remains ample ocular evidence to the pleasure he took in his borders during his ministry of five and thirty years. By him and his family the garden was greatly enriched with a pretty extensive collection of shrubs and herbaceous and alpine plants.

And now, in the person of the Rev. G. Wauchope Stewart the garden owns a new incumbent who is not too proud to take honest pride in fruits and flowers of his own raising, or to soil his hands with spade labour. Under his care and that of Mrs. Stewart there is no fear that the well-stocked garth will be impoverished or that the borders will be allowed to run wild. Much and sedulous attention is required, for the grounds are full of nooks and unexpected spaces, each with its store of choice things. Specially deserving of thoughtful tending is a bit of wall garden—" a garden of remembrance "—where saxifrages of many sorts, stonecrops, *Ramondia*, bellflowers, and other pretty flowers are well established —gifts from friends to the departed pastor and his family. Sure no fitter or more touching remembrance can be devised than these lowly herbs, for is not

---

[1] Mrs. Cruikshank is buried in the apse of the parish church between her two husbands.

a flower the true symbol of the resurrection? And does not each one, re-appearing season after season, seem to breathe the prayer—"Will ye no come back again?"

Before leaving Fyvie, leave should be obtained to enter the parish kirk to view a truly beautiful west window which has been placed there to the memory of Lord Leith of Fyvie's only son, a subaltern in the Royal Dragoons, who died in service in the South African war in 1900, aged only nineteen. This window is quite the most beautiful bit of modern stained glass I have seen in any country, and its effect is enhanced, if anything, by the surprise of finding such a fine work of art in a building which, externally, is very unpromising.

SUNDERLAND HALL

SELKIRKSHIRE

"'O the broom and the bonny, bonny broom,
    The broom o' the Cowdenknowes'—
And aye sae sweet as the lassie sang
    In the bucht milking the ewes."[1]

OW the old lilt ran in my head as I travelled one hot morning in June from Galashiels to Lindean, for the golden broom was in full glory on the river banks—such glory, that if it were a tender exotic, requiring careful coddling and nicety of soil, I think we should build glass houses for its accommodation, as now we do for costly orchids. Truly, it seemed vain to seek in garden ground for colour more pure or fragrance more perfect than were so lavishly offered in field and hedge and hanging copse, for what can excel the broom in splendour or the may-blossom in scent? Nor could there be devised a more charming contrast to the glowing gold of the broom than

[1] Southerners will miss the rhyme unless they follow the Scots in pronouncing "ewes" as "yows," for thus the sound of the Anglo-Saxon *eowu* has been pronounced in the northern dialect, as it has been in many other words.

139

the cool tint of field-geraniums, which sheeted the railway embankments with purple.

But Miss Wilson having set up her easel in the angle of land formed by the confluence of Ettrick Water with the Tweed, it was my business to follow and supplement with plodding pen the work of her swift pencil. My goal was Sunderland Hall, the pleasant abode of Mr. Scott Plummer, a modern mansion set in a park of ancient trees, with a garden that looks much older than the house. If it be a merit, and I hold it to be no slight one, that a garden should have a distinct character of its own, that merit may be justly claimed for the garden of Sunderland Hall. It is set upon the steep ground rising abruptly from the north side of the house. Here is none of that tiresome affectation which thrusts the garden proper out of sight and prepares a few formal borders as a set-off to the architect's design. The garden here is part and parcel of the dwelling, a suite of roofless apartments as it were, into which you can pass at any moment through a pretty gate of wrought iron, with no more trouble than going upstairs. Upstairs, however, you must go, for, as aforesaid, the ground is very steep, and is cut into a series of terraces, plentifully stocked with choice flowering plants in luxuriant health. The sense of moving through a suite of apartments is confirmed by the solid walls of clipped yew which sub-divide the slope in all directions, and by the carpet-like texture of the

140

SUNDERLAND HALL.

fine sward under foot. There are also retaining walls of stone, one of the delightful features which remain in memory being a fine specimen of the Austrian copper rose, whereof the brilliant garlands were charmingly set off by the grey masonry to which the plant is trained. It is a cruel misnomer that this fine briar is called "copper," for there is nothing metallic in the intense, yet velvety, glow of the petals. It is a rose unmatched in colour by any other, and would be far more commonly grown had not fashion decreed that persons of position (and others) must spend the sweet o' the year in sun-baked streets, thereby stimulating florists to the production of late-flowering varieties. It would be impossible to have clipped yew in better condition than those under charge of Mr. Harvey, the head gardener; and, forasmuch as experts differ as to the best seasons for clipping evergreens, persons whom it may concern may care to note that it is his practice to clip them in August. In the kitchen ground there is a feature which I have not seen elsewhere, namely, apple-trees closely planted and trained into an arch over-head, forming a long pergola. This must be a charming object when the trees are · in blossom, for the boughs form their own support, and there is none of that too obtrusive structure which mars the effect of many a pergola. Whether this method of training is culturally to be commended for the production of fruit, the present deponent cannot affirm; but perhaps that is of little account on upper Tweedside, which is a cold district, ill-suited for the orchard industry. Yet have apple-trees long been grown there, for Merlin the Wizard apostrophises one of them in a poem preserved in the *Black Book of Carmarthen*. After his flight from the field of Ardderyd (Arthuret, near Carlisle), where the Pagan cause was finally overthrown by the Christian leader Rydderch Hael, A.D. 573, Merlin took up his abode in the Caledonian Forest, and, after living there for "ten years and forty," was buried at Drummelzier, where Powsail Burn joins the Tweed. The following passage occurs in his lament for the lost cause.

"Sweet apple tree, growing by the river!
Whereof the keeper shall not eat of the fruit;
Before I lost my wits I used to be round its stem
With a fair, playful maid, matchless in slender shape."[1]

But it is a fatal thing to begin prosing about the memories, historic and prehistoric, of this Border country. Merlin is not the only wizard who has cast his spell upon it, for we are here upon the outskirts of Ettrick Forest, whereof Washington Irving, nursed among the pathless forests and broad rivers of the New World, received so chill an impression when he visited Walter Scott at Abbotsford.

"I gazed about me," he wrote, "for a time with mute surprise. I beheld a mere succession of grey, waving hills, line beyond line, as far as my eye could reach, monotonous in their aspect, and so destitute of trees that one could almost

[1] Vivien of the legend and of Tennyson's idyll.

see a stout fly walking along their outline; and the far-famed Tweed appeared a naked stream, between bare hills, without a tree or a thicket on its banks. And yet such had been the magic web of poetry and romance thrown over the whole, that it had a greater charm for me than the richest scenery I had ever beheld in England."

Yet Dorothy Wordsworth discerned in this landscape a physical charm of which her father was not sensible.

"In one very sweet part of the vale," she notes in her journal, "a gate crossed the road, which was opened by an old woman who lived in a cottage close to it. I said to her —'You live in a very pretty place.'—'Yes,' she replied, 'the water o' Tweed is a bonnie water.' The lines of the hills are flowing and beautiful; the reaches of the vale long. In some places appear the remains of a forest, in others you will see as lovely a combination of forms as any traveller who goes in search of the picturesque need desire, and yet perhaps without a single tree; or at least, if trees are there, they should be very few, and he shall not care whether they be there or not."

The "magic web" lies as close and glitters as fair as when these words were written nearly ninety years ago; and the same hands that wove it wrought the earliest stages in transforming the physical landscape. When Scott began planting trees at Abbotsford, almost every vestige of the Caledonian forest had vanished from Tweedside, and the land wore that naked aspect which disappointed Washington Irving. But no one visiting Tweeddale and Teviotdale nowadays can complain that they are treeless. Fine timber adorns the parks, broad woodlands clothe the slopes, and the silvan glories of the river side are such as Scott dreamt of, planned, but lived not to realise. For he was the pioneer of replanting; there, between Sunderland Hall and Galashiels, are the woods he reared with so much zeal and forethought; it is to him that the traveller owes, not only the intellectual charm of the Border land, but much of its scenic beauty also.

Waiting at the pretty little waterside station of Lindean for the train from Selkirk, one cannot but recall events which made that place the last scene in a gallant life. William, son of Sir James Douglas of Lothian, is known in history as the Knight of Liddesdale; but the prowess he displayed, not only against the English in the war of independence, but also on French battlefields, gained him also the prouder title of the Flower of Chivalry. He won back from the English the Douglas estates on the Border, but in 1346 he was taken prisoner at the battle of Durham, along with King David II., whose hot-headed folly in provoking that conflict went nigh to sacrificing for good and all the hard-won liberty of his country. For six years the Flower of Chivalry drooped in a dungeon of the Tower of London. Better had he drooped to death; for, despairing of freedom, he turned traitor, and bargained with King Edward for release, receiving broad lands in Annandale, which he was to hold as an open door for the passage of English armies.

Meanwhile another William Douglas had returned

144

to Scotland and became the champion of her cause. This was the son of Archibald "the Tineman," who was killed at Halidon Hill in 1333, when young William was made the ward of his godfather, the Knight of Liddesdale, and was sent to France to be educated. Returning in 1351 to take up his lordship (he afterwards became first Earl of Douglas), William found that the Flower of Chivalry had not only annexed a good deal of his ward's property, but had allowed his estates to be overrun by Englishmen. The Knight avoided meeting his godson ; but one day the young lord found him hunting in Ettrick forest, where he—the young lord—had sole right of the chase, inherited from his uncle the "good Sir James of Douglas," Bruce's right-hand man. No man knoweth what ensued. Certain it is that where two men bearing the name of William Douglas met, only one, and he the younger, rode away, leaving the elder stark in the greenwood. The place where the Knight fell, only a little way from Sunderland Hall, is called Williamhope to this day.[1]

They carried all that remained of the Flower of Chivalry down to Lindean Church, where the body rested that night ; which must serve as an excuse for so much irrelevancy on the part of him who has undertaken to write about gardens.

Loitering on the station platform, I came upon matter germane to horticulture, for I found the

---

[1] The suffix "hope," so common in this district, is the Norse equivalent of the Gaelic "glen."

stationmaster, another Mr. Harvey, to be a keen and skilful amateur. In his garden flourish many plants quite out of the common run, such as *Incarvillea delavayi, Primula denticulata* (masses of it), some very choice larkspurs, notably a pale blue one called "lifeguardsman," for which Mr. Harvey observed with a sigh that he had paid far more money than he ought. How many of us might make similar confession, had we the candour!

BALCASKIE

FIFE

HE glory of the garden at Balcaskie, like that at the neighbouring Balcarres, consists in its huge terraces, which command the same enchanting prospect of wood and water, field and firth, and the once bitterly hostile principality of Laudonia or Lothian. But the terrace work at Balcaskie has the double advantage over that at Balcarres of having been planned by a great master of architecture in the Jacobean style of his own day, and of having been softened by the lapse of more than two centuries. What Sir Robert Sibbald described in 1710 as "a very pretty new house, with all modish conveniences of terraces, park, and plainting [*sic*]," has now become a very pretty old house, and the terraces, once so painfully spick and span, have mellowed into tender greys and browns, with stains of lichen and velvet cushions of moss, mouldering here and there into hospitable chinks and crannies, where thoughtful hands have established thriving colonies of saxifrage, *Erinus* and other wall-loving herbs.

SCOTTISH GARDENS

Similarly, the house, which in the fifteenth century must have been but a pele tower of the ordinary type, owned by the family of Strang (whence was descended Sir Robert Strange, who engraved bank-notes for Prince Charlie), passing by marriage to a grandson of Moncrieff of that ilk, was sold in the seventeenth century to Sir William Bruce, architect of Charles II.'s Palace of Holyroodhouse, who transformed the fortalice of Balcaskie into a fair Jacobean manor house. His handiwork is easily recognised in the characteristic flanking towers and pavilions, the details of the mouldings, and especially in the wonderfully rich plaster-work of the ceilings, which rival the masterpieces of that kind of decoration in Holyrood. It was an age when the classical renaissance, having spent its force on the Continent, still flowed strongly in the northern realm ; in token whereof are ranged the busts of Roman emperors along the principal terrace, each on the top of a mighty buttress of the vertical wall. Nymphs, agreeably discoloured, fauns picturesquely chipped, haunt the surrounding groves, posed on pedestals beside the woodland paths ; nor shall you look in vain for *le petit dieu, dont les yeux sont cachés, mais les fesses à decouvert.*

Evidence of a genial climate abounds in the vegetation of these grounds. An enormous *Wistaria* trails its serpentine length along the south front of the house, where is also to be seen on this May morning a pretty picture, formed by a white fantail

BALCASKIE.

dove nesting in a myrtle trained to a height of twenty feet on the wall. On the lower terrace is an immense *Cornus (Benthamia) capitata* occupying the whole space between two buttresses. It flowers abundantly, as a rule, which, as Mr. George Cavendish would say, "is a rare thing and seldom to be seen"—in the north country, at least; but it appears to have reached the limit of old age, signs of which are apparent in its weakly growth and sparse foliage. *Cordyline (Dracœna) australis* appears perfectly hardy here, promising, when a little older, to present a feature peculiarly in harmony with the stately surroundings. *Phygelius capensis*, usually grown as a not very effective herbaceous perennial, has reached a height of twenty feet on a wall—an example well worth following in other gardens. The western staircase of the upper terrace is garlanded with the far-reaching sprays of that most generous of all clematis, *C. montana*, which pours cataracts of ivory flowers over the old stonework and makes the air redolent of incense like May-blossom.

Among the humbler herbs, nothing is so remarkable as the abundance and luxuriance of the great Christmas rose (*Helleborus niger var. maximus* or *altifolius*). This is mainly due to the special treatment accorded to it by Mr. Maule, the head gardener, who obtained a root of this, the finest of all the hellebores, many years ago from the late Miss Hope of Wardie Lodge. I likewise received a root at about the same time from the same source;

but it may serve to demonstrate the merit of sagacious treatment if I confess that, whereas my whole stock at the present time could be comfortably lodged in a single wheel-barrow, Mr. Maule can show you *tons* of healthy plants growing vigorously as a crop in the kitchen garden, besides having disposed of great quantities of roots during a long succession of years. He makes no secret of his treatment, which, put briefly, consists in deep preparation of rather stiff soil and abundance of well-decayed leaf mould (peat he does not recommend). When it is desired to propagate the stock, he takes up the roots towards the end of March, cuts off all long ends, which, if left untrimmed, cause the crowns to rot, and dibbles the slices in lines. Many persons who have been driven to despair in attempting to increase this and other varieties of Christmas rose, may find a way to success through following these simple instructions.

Balcaskie presents a rare and charming example of the union of architecture and horticulture, so seldom effectively carried out by modern designers.

BALCARRES

FIFE

HE annals of the house of Lindsay contain inexhaustible material for the weaver of magazine literature; yet when Robert Chambers, some seventy years ago, wrote for his *Edinburgh Journal* a paper entitled "A Pilgrimage to Balcarres," he had but little to tell about the great historic family to which that fine estate belongs. For him Balcarres owed its chief attraction to association with the memory of a very charming and accomplished woman, Lady Anne Lindsay,[1] a memory whereof, it must be admitted, the modern architect and landscape gardener between them have succeeded in obliterating most of the physical landmarks. The old castle has been so completely masked by recent additions, as to divest it, externally at least, of all venerable suggestion; while the grassy slopes where gentle Anne Lindsay tended

---

[1] Daughter of James, fifth Earl of Balcarres, and thirtieth Lord Lindsay of Crawford. Lady Anne married Andrew Barnard and died in 1825. Her eldest brother, great-grandfather of the present Earl of Crawford and Balcarres, succeeded as twenty-third Earl of Crawford in addition to the other titles.

her flowers have been buried under tons of terraces, stone-built, and scaled by exorbitant stairways, severing us for ever from the footprints of bygone generations.

A garden has been created in the grandiose style of the early Victorian era—the age when Wyatt and Paxton designed parks and palaces, and Disraeli and Bulwer-Lytton peopled them with appropriate characters. The centuries will touch and retouch these terraces into charm; as yet, the elaborate stone-work has weathered too few winters —gathered too little moss—to gratify the eye; while shadeless gravel walks, wide enough to admit a battalion of grenadiers in column of half-companies, make one sigh for

> Les sentiers ombreux
> Où s'égarent les amoureux.

A little group of blue hyacinths have had the temerity to establish themselves at the foot of one of the great terrace stairs—pretty wildings, seeming to dread detection and expulsion, yet giving one the same agreeable thrill that is conveyed by a nod of recognition in a crowded assembly of strangers.

Where the masonry ceases, clipped yew hedges begin—hundreds of yards of them, with far-spread, intricate designs in clipped box. Altogether the leafage submitted to the shears in each season must be measured in acres. One is thankful that a noble arbutus near the range of vine-houses, has escaped the tonsure. It is about 22 feet in height

152

BALCARRES.

and measures 125 feet round the circumference of its branches. An inspiring point of brilliancy was furnished by the finest clump of *Adonis vernalis* I ever saw, whereon were blazing between thirty and forty satellites to the glorious May sun, testifying to what soil and climate in the East Neuk are capable of producing for spring display, were they but given a fair chance. According to present arrangements, all effort is focussed upon autumnal splendour, when, as shown in Miss Wilson's study, there is no lack of colour on walls and in parterres.

My visit to Balcarres was ill-timed for garden effect; outside there was ample beauty to compensate for flowerless borders, for it would be hard to find a more glorious bit of park scenery. Wych elm and sycamore, trees which must turn the century before attaining majesty, abound here of great size; there is also much fine ash timber, and some well-grown modern conifers, not scattered as specimens, but crowded as they should be in close forest. The Californian *Pinus monticola*, which is but a glorified form of the Weymouth pine, luxuriates here, and shows as yet no liability to the disease which has proved so fatal to this fine tree at Murthly. Dominating the whole demesne is Balcarres Craig, a lofty precipitous rock, from the summit of which a soul-stirring prospect spreads around. Beyond the rich woods and fertile plain lies the blue Firth of Forth, bearing on its bosom the massive Bass Rock. The smooth outline of the Lammermuir forms the southern horizon, within which Auld Reekie rears her dusky canopy.

A word about Lady Anne Lindsay, whose best years had sped before she changed her name in marrying Mr. Barnard. "Her hand," says her nephew, Colonel Lindsay, "was sought in marriage by several of the first men of the land, and her friendship and confidence by the most distinguished women ; but indecision was her failing ; hesitation and doubt upset her judgment ; her heart had never been captured, and she remained single till late in life, when she married an accomplished, but not wealthy, gentleman, younger than herself, whom she accompanied to the Cape of Good Hope when appointed Colonial Secretary under Lord Macartney."

Upon Scottish hearts this lady has founded an undying claim as the author of *Auld Robin Gray*, whereof Sir Walter Scott wrote as "that real pastoral which is worth all the dialogues which Corydon and Phyllis have had together, from the days of Theocritus downwards." The real authorship of this ballad, which from its first appearance in 1771 captured and retained the fancy of people of all ranks and many nationalities, was disputed for many years as hotly as that of *Waverley*. Strange to say it was the author of *Waverley* himself who first revealed the author of *Auld Robin Gray*, by comparing the lot of Minna in *The Pirate* to that of Jeanie Gray, "the village heroine in Lady Anne Lindsay's beautiful ballad."

BALCARRES

Nae langer she wept; her tears were a' spent;
Despair it was come, and she thought it content;
She thought it content, but her cheek it grew pale,
And she drooped like a snowdrop broke down by the hail.

For more than fifty years the secret had been kept, and when at last it was thus laid bare in 1823, Lady Anne disdained to disown the offspring of her Muse. Less than two years before her death, she wrote a full confession to Sir Walter, explaining how she had composed the verses to suit an old Scottish air of which she was "passionately fond," and had borrowed from the old herdsman of Balcarres the name of Robin Gray. Her letter, and Sir Walter's reply (both of which well repay perusal) are too long to print here. They are given in full in Lord Lindsay's delightful work, *The Lives of the Lindsays* (vol. ii. pp. 391-399).

"I have sometimes wondered," wrote Sir Walter in a later letter, "how many of our best songs have been written by Scotchwomen of rank and condition. The Hon. Mrs. Murray (Miss Baillie Jerviswood born) wrote the very pretty Scots song

'An't were not my heart's light I wad die,'—

Miss Elliot of Minto, the verses of the *Flowers o' the Forest* which begin

'I've heard a lilting,' etc.—

Mrs. Cockburn composed other verses to the same tune,

'I have seen the smiling of fortune's beguiling,' etc.—

Lady Wardlaw wrote the glorious old ballad of *Hardyknute*. Place *Auld Robin* at the head of this list, and I question if we masculine wretches can claim five or six songs equal in elegance and pathos out of the long list of Scottish minstrelsy."

CARNOCK

T would be difficult, if not impossible, to find a more characteristic example of Scottish domestic architecture of the sixteenth and seventeenth centuries than that presented in the old house of Carnock. Originally built in 1548 by Sir Robert Drummond, whose arms and initials, with those of his wife, Margaret Elphinstone of Dunmore, still remain over the principal entrance, it was added to in 1634 when the property was acquired by Sir Thomas Nicolson, and remains unchanged in its main features, though outbuildings and offices have been erected to adapt the dwelling to the require-ments of a modern household.

"'What a distance," observed Messrs. M'Gibbon and Ross, " has been travelled over in the three centuries which have elapsed from the time when Scottish nobles were content to live in towers containing three apartments only—a ground floor for cattle, a first floor for a hall in which the retainers lived and slept, and a top storey for the lord and his family! The introduction of a kitchen was at first hailed as an im-

156

CARNOCK.

portant innovation and improvement, all provisions having been previously cooked in the hall or in the open air. But in the seventeenth century people have become so refined that the kitchen, with what was formerly considered its sweet perfumery, must be banished out of doors. The domestics are now quite separated from the hall, while the proprietor and his family, no longer huddled up in one room, enjoy the delights of the modern dining-room and drawing-room, private sitting-rooms and bedrooms, all provided with separate doors."[1]

Those who sigh for the good old times and repine because their lot was not cast "in days of old when knights were bold," may incline to think that the domestic discomfort of a sixteenth century Scottish mansion is exaggerated in the passage above-quoted. They may agree that the knight and his family dined at the same table with the servants; what could be more picturesque and in keeping with feudal custom? But surely the lady had her bower, where she worked embroidery with her maidens, while a pretty page or sadly attired clerk read aloud some romaunt of chivalry—say the stirring adventures of Ferambras and Oliver or the story of Sir Eglamour of Artois. She would also have her parterres, spending much of her time in tending her favourite flowers. Alas! if you would learn the naked truth from an eye-witness, hear how Fynes Moryson described his entertainment in a Scottish country house of the seventeenth century.

"My self was at a Knight's house, who had many servants to attend him, that brought in his meate with their heads

[1] *Castellated and Domestic Architecture of Scotland,* ii. 496.

covered with blew caps, the Table being more then halfe furnished with great platters of porredge, each having a little peece of sodden meate; And when the Table was served, the servants did sit downe with us, but the upper messe in steede of porredge, had a Pullet with some prunes in the broth. And I observed no Art of Cookery, or furniture of Houshold stuffe, but rather rude neglect of both, though my selfe and my companion, sent from the Governour of Barwicke about bordering affaires, were entertained after their best manner. . . . Their bedsteads were like Cubbards in the wall, with doores to be opened and shut at pleasure, so as we climbed up to our beds. They use but one sheete, open at the sides and top, but close at the feete, and so doubled." [1]

It may well be imagined that, luxury being so scant within doors, little care was bestowed in furnishing the garden with anything except kitchen stuff; but when I was last at Carnock ample amends had been made in that respect by the lady of the castle, who is an enthusiastic gardener. The property passed to the Shaw Stewarts by marriage in the eighteenth century; the present Sir Hugh and Lady Alice lived at Carnock till he succeeded his father in 1903, when they moved to Ardgowan and let the old house. I know not what may be the appearance of that garden now, but half-a-dozen years ago it was a joy to behold. Every border overflowed with blossom; alpine *Erinus*, saxifrages and other clinging herbs clustered in crevices of the old walls and in the chinks of the broad stone

[1] *Itinerary*, iv. 183 [ed. 1908]. Moryson's visit to Scotland took place between 1605 and 1617.

steps on the terrace front. There was abundance and luxuriance of Christmas roses such as one may seldom enjoy; for the purpose of this garden was not to produce a culminating blaze at the end of the London season, such as was deemed the acme of mid-Victorian horticulture, but to link season with season and month with month by a succession of blossom. No flower is more important to this scheme than the varieties of *Helleborus niger*. The torch lilies have not quenched their flames nor the late asters their stars before the variety called *maximus* or *altifolius* unfurls its great blooms, tinted like apple-blossom, to be followed about Christmas-tide by *major*, Madame Fourcade, *angustifolius* and others, which choose the darkest, dreariest time of the whole year for their display, and keep things going till snowdrops, aconites and crocus strike the first chord in the overture of another year.

Simple as the requirements of Christmas roses, it is a fact that failures are more frequent than success in its cultivation. Many an amateur, delighted with the rare sight of a mass of ivory blooms, rose-tinted on the backs, resolves to have the like in his own garden, so that Christmas roses ought to be as commonly seen in good condition as double daisies or daffodils. But they are not: a luxuriant bank of *Helleborus niger* is one of the rarest sights in horticulture. I have been gardening for forty years and more, yet have never yet succeeded to my liking with these charming flowers. Coming,

coming, coming—but never yet come. Yet we are assured that all they want is deep loam, partial shade and to be let alone. One precaution must not be neglected in gardens where pheasants come— namely, to surround the bed with wire-netting before they come into flower, else will these greedy birds nip off every bud.[1]

[1] I leave this as it was written after my last visit to Carnock, because I feel sure that my experience has its parallel in that of many other amateurs. But in the paper on Balcaskie (p. 149) I have described how Mr. Maule, the gardener there, instructed me in the right management and propagation of hellebore.

KELBURNE CASTLE

AYRSHIRE

N all the west no fairer prospect can be had than is commanded by one standing above the pretty little watering place of Fairlie on the Firth of Clyde. I have studied it at all seasons and in all moods of weather: beshrew me if I can tell which becomes it best—a clear winter day, when the fantastic fairyland of Arran gleams snow-clad beyond the blue-waters in almost unreal splendour —a summer morning, when the sea lies pearly calm and the eastern rays reveal every glen and corrie, every shattered peak and shadowed cliff in the brotherhood of Goat Fell,—or again in September, when that outline whereof the eye never wearies is cast in purple, clear-cut silhouette against the saffron west, while the dusky isles of Cumbrae and Bute fill in the quiet middle distance. In all its aspects it is a perfect landscape, and although the lord who built his tower in the sixteenth century on the brink of Kelburne Glen, may have had in view strategic rather than æsthetic considerations, it happened here, as it has happened in many another instance, that both purposes were best secured on the same site.

The central tower of Kelburne Castle is dated 1581. It may have been built—probably was so—on the site of an earlier keep—but it was not many years old when Timothy Pont, to whom we owe such an intimate knowledge of Scottish topography before the union of the Crowns, described it in the following words.

"Kelburne Castell, a goodly building veill planted, hauing werey beutiful orchards and gardens and in one of them a spatious Rome adorned with a chrystalin fontane cutte all out of the living rocke. It belongs heretably to Johne Boll [Boyle] Laird thereof."

The gardens remain, enriched with the dignity that only centuries can confer; but the "spatious Rome [? room]"—where is it? Miss Wilson's drawing shows a circular stone basin, wherein stands, not a fountain, but a wonderful sundial, wrought, apparently, by the same hand as one dated 1707 which stands near the house. The surmise of the present "Boll"—to wit, David, seventh Earl of Glasgow—is that when David, the first Earl, was adding to the house and had the dated sundial erected there, he was so well pleased with it that he had a second one made and substituted it for the "chrystalin fontane." Be that as it may, one has no reason to complain of the result, so admirably does this old dial, stained and mellowed by the time which it was set there to measure, harmonise with

KELBURNE CASTLE.

the old-world borders, the paths of smooth sward and the ancient yews which seem to set time at defiance. Nobody now notes the shadow of the gnomon, for every man carries a time-keeper in his pocket, and ladies, who have no pockets, bind untrustworthy watches on their wrists or pin them on their bosoms; but we are none of us the worse of the warning conveyed by this grey column in a pleasure ground, which seems to echo the old Scots saw—

"Tak' tent o' time ere time be tynt."[1]

A charming example is Kelburne of Scots building of the sixteenth century, the original tower of "Johne Boll" standing clear, unimpaired, and unmutilated by the first Earl's addition. On the south-west front of it is the old herb garth enclosed in high walls, now converted into a pleasaunce, with flower beds and shrubberies lying fair to the sun, with the broad waters of the firth shimmering beyond. Shady alleys run round the enclosure, not laid with crunchy gravel but with greensward of seductive texture, bordered with shrubs, among which are just so many of the choicer kinds to cause one to wish for more. *Rhododendron Thomsoni* and *campanulatum* are each over 12 feet high; the common myrtle forms a great bush without the protection of a wall; samples these of what a rare collection might be ranged here if some of the common stuff were cleared away. In one of the gardens in the town of Fairlie I noticed *Cordyline*

[1] Take heed of time ere it be beyond recall.

163

australis twenty feet high; what then might not be made of this fine enclosure with its kindly sheltering walls if the space occupied by aucuba and clipped Portugal laurel were devoted to some of the host of lovely things that delight in a western climate—such as *Carpenteria, Desfontainea, Eucryphia* and Himalayan rhododendrons? Also one grudges the wall space covered with masses of ivy, for the masonry might be draped with many forms of beauty, too tender to stand alone.

A curious enclosure, some thirty feet square, with high walls, stands at one corner of this pleasaunce. It is roofless now, but appears to have been once a pavilion or large summer house. The entrance is through a pretty wicket of wrought iron, and the interior is occupied by Lady Glasgow's rock garden, a delightful nook for the cultivation of choice flowers and ferns. The more modern kitchen garden has broad borders backed with rose-covered pergolas and filled with a general herbaceous collection, well-ordered and in excellent condition. Conspicuous in early July were two varieties of dittany (*Dictamnus fraxinella*) of a brighter rose tint than I have seen elsewhere, a great improvement on the ordinary type, which is not very satisfactory in colour. A bright myosotis was very pleasing. I took it at first for the hybrid of *azorica* named "Imperatrice Elizabeth," but the gardener informed me it was called "Queen Victoria."

Before going up the glen one pauses to admire a

splendid specimen of *Pinus insignis*, of unusually erect and graceful habit. Judged by the eye, it must be between 90 and 100 feet high, and the tape gave its girth as 15 feet at 4 feet above the ground. Among all the pines there is none to be so highly prized as this for its dense, rich green foliage, distinguishing it in winter from every other evergreen.

The glen is one of the chief attractions of the place, though here again one longs to substitute tree ferns and rare rhododendrons for some of the tangle of *R. ponticum* and native undergrowth. The burn has tunnelled its way through the soft red sandstone close to the house; a natural cascade fills the air with ceaseless sound—a gentle tinkle in summer heats, a thunderous rush in autumn spates. Paths line the cliffs on either side the stream: one of them leads to a grove of lofty silver firs, amid which is set a tablet to the memory of John, Earl of Glasgow (d. 1755), to the narrative of whose prowess some ambiguity is imparted by uncertainty of punctuation. Thus—

> "At the Battle of Fontenoy Early in Life,
> he lost his Hand and his Health His
> Manly Spirit, not to be subdued, at Lafield
> he received Two Wounds in one Attack."

Lord Glasgow observes a commendable practice in displaying his own arms from the flagstaff on the tower, and nobly does the scarlet eagle, double-headed on a yellow field, flaunt in the breeze, in high relief against a dark background of hanging woods. It would add greatly to the interest of a countryside were other landowners to follow his example, each hoisting the heraldic bearings to which he is entitled; for deeply as we revere the flag which is famed (with scant historical accuracy) for having "braved a thousand years the battle and the breeze," it loses some of its significance when it is flown from any public house or tea-garden.

CULZEAN

HREE hundred years ago, probably the last place in the realm that any student of horticulture would choose for his tranquil vocation would be that lofty bluff on the Firth of Clyde whereon stands Culzean Castle,[1] for this was of old the stronghold of a branch of the Kennedys—the most powerful and turbulent clan in south-western Scotland after the fall of the Black Douglas.

> " From Wigtown to the toun of Ayr,
>   Portpatrick to the Cruives o' Cree,
>   Nae man need think for to bide there
>   Unless he ride wi' Kennedy."

Culzean remains to this day the principal residence of the Marquess of Ailsa, head of the clan ; and, forasmuch as the zest of tranquillity and order is greatly enhanced by contrast with the insecurity of an elder time, it may be permitted to admit the reader to a glimpse of the state of society when the Kennedys were a formidable power in the land,

---

[1] It is pronounced Cullàne.

167

by quoting from an anonymous chronicle of the family composed towards the end of the sixteenth century.[1] It relates how Gilbert Kennedy, fourth Earl of Cassilis, acquired the lands of the Abbey of Crosraguel.

"This last Gilbertt was ane particuler manne and ane werry greidy manne, and cairitt nocht how he gatt land, sa that he culd cum be [come by] the samin. . . . He conquessit the abbacy be this forme. Thair was ane fader-broder [uncle] of his callit Abbot Quinteyne, ane gud manne and ane that feiritt God, efter the maner of religione. At the alteratioune of the religioun[2] my lord deltt with the abbott and gut the few [obtained the freehold] of the said abbacy sett to him; bot the samin wes querrellit [repudiated] be the nixt intrant abbot. . . And then ane abott, Allane Stewart, gatt the abbacy; and this abott had mareyitt ane sister of the Lady Barganyis, and followitt his opinione in all his adois [doings]. My Lord of Caissillis, perseiffing the samin, desyrit the Laird of Bargany[3] to mowe [move] the abbott to conferme his rycht, sett be the Abott Quinteyne of befoir. Bot the Laird culd nocht gett the abott mowitt [moved] to cum to him, that he mycht deill with him. . . Quhairupone the laird persuadit the abott and sent him to Mayboll to my lord. Att quhais [whose] cuming, my lord delt with him to ratifie his rycht; bot could nocht gett him mowitt thairto. Quhairupon he tuik purpoise to conwoy him to Dounour [Dunure], and thair to mowe him to do the samin be violens. And quhane [when] he fand [found] him obstinatt,

---

[1] *The Historie of the Kennedyis*: supposed to have been compiled by John Mure of Auchendrane while awaiting his decapitation, to which, with his son, he was condemned for the murder of Sir Thomas Kennedy of Culzean in 1597, and for several other horrible crimes.

[2] The Reformation.   [3] Kennedy of Bargany was a near kinsman of Earl Gilbert's.

at last tuik him and band him to ane furme [form], and sett
his bair legis to ane gritt fyr, and extreymly brunt him,
that he was ewer thairefter onabill of his leggis."

Such is the chronicler's succinct account of the
roasting of the Abbot of Crosraguel; to realise the
full extent of the Earl's heartlessness one should
peruse this unhappy cleric's petition to the Privy
Council for redress. At the first roasting, on 1st
September, 1570, the Abbot consented to renounce
his lands, but on the 7th, being asked to sign a
document giving effect to the renunciation, he
vowed he would rather die ; whereupon his tormentor
ordered the fire to be re-lighted, and his wretched
victim to be trussed for a second ordeal.

"Then," declared the abbot, "being in so grit paine as I
truste never man was in. . . I cried, 'Fye vpon you ! will ye
ding whingaris [thrust swords] in me and put me out of this
world ? or elis put a barell of poulder vnder me, rather nor
to be demaned [treated] in this vnmercifull maner ?' The
said erle, hearing me cry, bade his servant Alexander
Ritchart put ane serviat [napkin] in my throat, which he
obeyed. . . wha then, seing that I was in danger of my life,
my flesch consumed and brunt to the bones, and that I wald
not condescend to thair purpose, I was releivit of that paine ;
whairthrow I uill never be able nor weill in my lifetime."

The brave abbot was rescued from duresse by
another Kennedy, laird of Bargany, and carried off
to Ayr, "brunt as he was." Cassilis got off pretty
cheap. Being too powerful a chief to offend with
safety, he was bound over to keep the peace

x   169

towards the abbot under £2000 Scots, equal to £177 13s. 4d. sterling.

This gentle episode was but one in a long series of ghastly outrages—arson, murder, mutilation, and the like—perpetrated by rival septs of the Kennedys upon each other and upon their neighbours. In the year preceding the union of the Crowns John, fifth Earl of Cassilis, Lord Treasurer of Scotland, set his hand to the following document, which is preserved in the charter chest at Barnbarroch, and is remarkable even according to the practice of those violent times as being uttered by a Minister of the Crown.

"WE, Johnne erle of Cassillis, lord Kennedy, &c., bindis and oblissis ws that, howsovnne [so soon as] our broder Hew Kennedy of Brounstone, with his complices, taikis the laird of Auchindraneis lyf that we sall maik guid and thankfull payment to him and thame of the sowme of tuelff hundreth merkis[1] yeirly, togidder with corne to sex horsis, ay and quhill [so long as] we ressave thame in houshald with our self, beginning the first payment immediatlie efter thair committing of the said deid.

ATTOUR, howsovnne we ressave thame in houshald, we sall pay to the twa serving gentillmen the feis yeirlie as our awin [own] houshald gentillmen, and heirto we obliss ws vpone our honour.

Subscryvit with our hand AT Maybole the ferd [third] day of September 1602.   JOHNE ERLE OF CASSILLIS."

With such echoes of an age not very remote ringing in one's ears, it is difficult to realise that

[1] Equal to £800 Scots or £66 13s. 4d. sterling.

CULZEAN.

this garden by the sea is the very scene of many episodes of a blood feud which raged for more than a hundred years, and cost many Scotsmen, gentle and simple, their lives.

The lofty bluff whereon the castle stands has doubtless been a fortified position from prehistoric times. It is inaccessible on the west, where the cliff falls sheer to the sea, and the ground slopes sharply away inland to the east, where a natural gully, originally deepened for defensive purposes, has been cast into a couple of walled terraces forming a delectable abode for many shrubs which cannot face an inland winter. The peculiar conformation of the ground affords that shelter from blustering winds and salt-laden gales which so often neutralise the genial influence of the sea side. At the foot of the terraces is a broad, well-shaven lawn, with a fountain and architectural basin in the centre, and plenty of room for a couple of tennis courts besides.

These tennis courts have become permanently marked out in a curious manner which I have not noted elsewhere. The lines drawn in whitewash during several successive seasons have killed the grass, which has been replaced by a strong growth of daisies. The mowing machine of course prevents these from flowering, but their flat shining leaves, darker than the surrounding grass, distinctly show the limits of the courts, so as to render unnecessary any fresh measurement when the nets are set out in summer. If it were possible to grow the aucuba-leaved daisy

171

with sufficient certainty in the turf, players need desire no painted lines. That pretty daisy is rather fickle in behaviour; but perhaps it would respond to the stimulus of lime applied in a wash, which has had such a remarkable effect on the common green-leaved kind. One of the first plants to attract attention on the terrace walls is the violet abutilon (*Abutilon vitifolium*), which grows twelve feet high, presenting a lovely spectacle when covered with its large flowers in June and July. The rare and tender *Olearia Fosteri* is quite happy here, sheltered by broad curtains of common myrtle and several species of *Escallonia. Drymis winteri*, also, grows robustly, producing fine trusses of fragrant white flowers early in the year, and perfecting its glossy foliage in the sunshine which floods every corner of the terraces and lawns.

On the whole, however, these terraces, so ample in their proportions, so admirably suited in their south-easterly aspect for the culture of rare exotics, have not yet been turned to full account, as doubtless they soon will be, for their owner, the Marquess of Ailsa, constantly resides in the home of his ancestors, and is an enthusiastic and skilful amateur. Moreover, he is fortunate in his head gardener, Mr. Murray, who, both by knowledge and inclination, is well qualified for the charge of an extensive collection of exotics. Much of the wall space is occupied by plants which will thrive in any garden; but these are being gradually removed to make way for choicer

172

things, whereof a very rich collection is being raised in the kitchen garden. That garden, a spacious enclosure within brick walls, lies about a quarter of a mile south of the castle, well sheltered by lofty beech woods and approached through an avenue of splendid silver firs. This tree, the loftiest European species, seldom receives the treatment of close canopy required to bring it to perfection. It is usually seen isolated or at wide intervals in mixed plantation, where its head, towering above all others, becomes ragged and bent by the prevailing winds. Moreover, unlike others of the genus *Abies*, it is a shade-bearer; hence, unless it be grown in dense mass, it throws out a multitude of strong side branches, which ruins the timber, naturally of fine quality. In this avenue the firs stand in close rank, their silvery boles rising straight and clean, a truly beautiful sight when the sunbeams slant through the dark canopy overhead. The largest of these trees has reached a height of 120 feet, with a circumference of 15 feet at 4 feet from the ground.

In the garden itself, attention is first claimed for things of mature growth. A single plant of *Rhododendron ponticum* measures 243 feet in circumference and 21 feet high, and, when in full flower, shows what a truly splendid thing is this common shrub, so often vulgarised by use in the wrong place. It may surprise many people to see *Buddleia colvillei* already four feet high, flowering freely in the open border without any protection in winter. On the far

side of a grove of *Cordyline australis,* some of them
15 feet high with the blossoming branches faded, is
a bank set with *Romneya coulteri,* a noble company.
It is a question whether this fine poppywort should
not be cut to the ground after flowering and allowed
to spring again. This is not done at Culzean, and the
flowers, though very numerous, are not individually
so large as those produced on young growths. At
one end of this bank is a mass of the Kerguelen
Island cabbage (*Myosotidium nobile*) which, though it
flowers and seeds abundantly, shows no symptom of
that failure which has overtaken it in so many
gardens. *Rodgersia podophylla* makes a luxuriant
undergrowth in the shrubberies, with enormous leaves
turning in August to bronze and copper tints.

Among the young stock note may be made of
healthy plants of *Leucodendron argenteum, Senecio
rotundifolius, Eleagnus marginata, Enkyanthus japonicus*
with waxy flowers in early summer, and deep red
leaves in autumn, *Hydrangea involucrata,* of which
the half-expanded trusses resemble huge blue moss-
roses, *Berberis congestiflora,* with remarkably fine
foliage, *Mitraria coccinea,* and many other rare plants,
which Mr. Murray finds no difficulty in rearing in
the open till they are of a size to plant out in
the grounds.

Passing now into the woodland beyond the
garden, where Miss Wilson has chosen her subject,
Lord Ailsa's full design becomes manifest, namely, to
devote these glades and glens and the margin of a

fine sheet of water so as to develop the natural character of hardy exotics set free in a Scottish environment. It would take much space to describe the many objects of interest in this wide demesne. Mention may be made of the luxuriant growth of tree-ferns (*Dicksonia antarctica*), many of which are six and eight feet high with far-spreading fronds. It is to be hoped that some enterprising nurseryman will set himself to propagate these noble cryptogams, which are far hardier than many people suppose, though very impatient of exposure to burning sun and high winds. The supply is severely limited at present, owing to the timely and commendable action of the New Zealand Government in prohibiting the exportation of these ferns, which were in danger of being exterminated by collectors.

Many of the bamboos in this wild garden flowered themselves to death in the summers of 1905 and 1906, notably *Arundinaria simoni*, but many hundreds of seedlings have been raised to take their place, albeit it requires some trouble to protect from small birds the sweet grain produced by these giant grasses.

One specially beautiful shrub claims notice before leaving a glade set with *Cordyline* and tree ferns, to wit, *Myrtus* (*Eugenia*) *apiculata*. Fully seven feet high, set with panicles of bell-shaped fragrant blossoms, like rose-tinted ivory, the question which naturally suggests itself is, why is such a charming shrub, flowering in August and September, not more commonly planted?

SCOTTISH GARDENS

Of the interior of the great castle of the Kennedys, its spacious saloons and well-furnished armoury, this is not the place to treat; but it may be observed in passing from it that nothing could be less applicable to it at the present day than the description given by the Parliamentarian commander, Sir William Brereton, who, having occasion to lodge at Culzean during the civil war, has the following note about his quarters:

"A pretty, pleasantly-seated house or castle, which looks full upon the main sea. Hereunto we went, and there found no hall, only a dining-room or hall, a fair room, and almost as large as the whole pile, but very sluttishly kept; unswept; dishes, trenchers and wooden cups thrown up and down, and the room very nasty and unsavoury."

Reckoning one thing against another, perhaps we have less reason than some people would have us believe to regret the passing of the good old times.

LECKIE

HE old house of Leckie stands about six miles west of Stirling on that fair wooded slope which makes the foot-hills of the precipitous Lennox range, separating it from the flat Carse of Menteith, through which lowland Forth, deep-cradled in willowy banks, winds her eastward way to meet her Highland sister, impetuous Teith. Apt emblems, these two rivers, of the two races of men whose confines lay along their course of yore. The Teith, poured from the great lochs of Vennachar and Lubnaig, rushes out upon the plain with as much tumult as did of old the Highland caterans, swarming from mountain and glen to drive a prey: the Forth—silent, sullen, profound—flows with scarcely perceptible current, yet moves as resistlessly as men of Saxon blood to the appointed end.

A beautiful old house, designed for that combination of domestic ease with defensive qualities that was the aim of Scottish architects in the hazardous reign of Queen Mary. On the east side

Y   177

a wing has been thrown out to meet the more exacting requirements of the eighteenth century; but even that did not serve to satisfy a modern household, and in the nineteenth century a brand new mansion was erected; the ancient home, with all its chequered association, was evacuated, the green "pleuse" and flowery borders were ploughed up, and the old house was applied to the accommodation of workmen and their families.

Yet it was not upon the fine new terraces or among the flaunting parterres that Miss Wilson's choice of a subject fell, but under the time-worn walls, where a few flowers still linger, though the former inmates have passed away. The house, so far as it is inhabited, now serves for a working man's dwelling; and readers may be disposed to dispute its claim for a place among Scottish gardens. Indeed, it affords no example of successful cultivation. The flowers are but those whose constitution enables them to survive neglect and run wild; but the drawing illustrates so well those gleams and flashes of colour which we sometimes see reflected from a forgotten past, that I could not find it in my heart to put it aside.

In this instance the colour comes from two species of Tropæolum—namely, the annual Indian Cress (*T. nasturtium*), and the perennial *T. speciosum*, which cottagers sometimes call, by easy transposition of consonants, the "petroleum plant." Both of these are natives of South America, and, like many others

LECKIE.

from the same region, adapt themselves with remarkable readiness to the cool soil and humid air of the north. The exquisite beauty of the perennial species, with its delicate leafage, festoons of carmine blossom and blue berries, has been the despair of many English amateurs; for there are very few places south of Yorkshire where it will consent to flourish. Yet it is very capricious; establishing itself sometimes in the most unexpected way and in the least likely environment. Thus in Mrs. Benson's beautiful garden at Buckhurst in Sussex, on a dry, hot soil, this tropæolum has possessed itself of some of the borders, over-running shrubs and walls as wantonly and irresistably as in any Scottish cottage garden.

Leckie, like most places in this central plain of Scotland, is rich in historic association. It belonged once to King Robert the Bruce, who, in 1326, gave half the lands to his ancient ally Malcolm, Earl of Lennox, receiving in exchange two plough-gates of land at Cardross on the Clyde,[1] where he built himself a country house and spent his declining years in the usual pursuits of a country gentleman—hunting, hawking, farming and yachting. It was at Leckie that Prince Charlie lay after Lord George Murray had routed General Hawley at Falkirk. It was the last house he occupied in the Lowlands, setting forth thence in the dark days of January, 1746, on his ill-starred march to the north, where his star was to be quenched for evermore on Culloden Moor.

---

[1] Not Cardross on the Forth, which is only a few miles east of Leckie.

DALZELL CASTLE

T is told of a distinguished Frenchman who applied himself resolutely to master the anomalies of English orthography and pronunciation, that he made famous progress with ordinary vocables such as "cough" and "plough," "read" and "bread," the verb "sow" and the substantive "sow," etc. ; but had to confess himself gravelled among proper names. "Here," he complained, "is a gentleman who spells his name C-H-O-L-M-O-N-D-E-L-E-Y, and you tell me it sounds 'Marchbanks!' But it is not reasonable, that!"

Equally deceitful is the pitfall dug for the southerner who mispronounces the name Dalzell according to its spelling, or, as he or she may feel disposed to put it, pronounces it according to the misspelling. The correct pronunciation is attained simply by naming the consonants D L, with stress on the L. "Then, why on earth," grumbles the English visitor, "cannot Scotsmen spell names as they wish them pronounced?" To which fair rejoinder might be made by referring to such English names as Worcester, Cirencester, etc. ; only that is the *tu quoque*

DALZELL.

form of argument—scarcely courteous, I trow; so it may be explained that in the old Scottish alphabet the character z did not represent the soft sibilant as in "zebra," but the consonantal y, as in "youth," to distinguish it from the vowel y, as in "syllable." If you press me further and inquire how "Dal" can fairly be supposed to represent the sound "dee," I am driven to retort that it is no whit more absurd than to write "Pontefract" when you mean one to read "Pomfret." So we start fair, you see: and having settled that point, let us look into Lord Hamilton's pretty Clydeside garden.

It is formed in terraces cut in the steep side of a deep and rocky gorge, through which a burn brawls impatiently to join the sweeping Clyde. Quoth William Cobbett, who paid a visit to Dalzell in 1832, "Here, were I compelled to live in Scotland, would I choose to reside." Since that time seventy— nearly eighty—years have run, to the mighty detriment of the atmosphere; for the development of mining, smelting, and malodorous industries in variety has greatly altered for the worse the aspect of this part of Clydesdale. Scarcely would Sir Walter Scott recognise the groves round neighbouring Cambusnethan, where there is a railway station, solemnly placarded as "Tillietudlem," in compliance with the unconscious decree of the Wizard of the North.

But what Dalzell has lost in environment it has gained in the charm of contrast. You step off the tram midway between the busy hives of Motherwell and Wishaw, enter the park gate, and you have not passed far beneath an avenue of limes before you have exchanged an atmosphere pulsating with industry and pungent with its waste products into one vibrating with the song of birds and redolent of hawthorn and lilac. On the way to the flower garden you pass some fine trees—notably, an immense oak close to the castle. It separates into several great branches at ten feet above the ground, and is not remarkable for height; but it contains an enormous bulk of solid timber, the bole *at its narrowest part* measuring twenty-four feet in girth. It is a deceptive tree in one respect. At first sight I judged it to be of the sessile-flowered variety, which is the prevailing native form in the western districts of Scotland; and this impression was confirmed by the fact that the leaves were set on foot-stalks. But closer inspection showed that the flowers were also on long foot-stalks, that the leaves had "auricles" or little rounded flaps at the base, and that they were perfectly smooth on the back, without the pubescence which the sessile oak invariably has in greater or less quantity. This tree, therefore, belongs undoubtedly to the pedunculate race.

The flower garden is set on the terraces on the south side of the house, and very charming it is, with a happy combination of formality and freedom. Miss Wilson has chosen her subject on the upper terrace, when the Dutch borders, deeply bordered with box, were aglow with begonias. I followed her in early summer, before the bedding out had taken effect, but there was plenty to please the eye and awaken interest. The terrace walls were so beautifully embroidered in parts with aubrietia, rock-roses, arabis, wall-flowers, saxifrages, dianthus, and such like, which had been inserted as seedlings in the chinks of the masonry, and had grown into hanging cushions, that one could not but wish that some of the ivy, of which there is over-much to please a gardener, might be cleared off in favour of choicer growths.

The terrace stairs are neither prim nor kept too scrupulously bare. On the contrary, saxifrages, bell-flowers and yellow corydalis enliven every step and joint, with here a springing fern or foxglove, and there a hanging clematis. There is just enough alluring disarray to soften the architectural preciseness of the design.

The lower terrace is even more delightful, for here a broad grass walk is laid between two long herbaceous borders. Woad tosses its golden spray amid troops of iris, and woodruff wafts its delicate incense from every waste corner. And to complete the charm, the sound of running water is ever in one's ears, rising from the burn far below, where, in a grassy glade, *Gunnera* spreads her broad sails, to be viewed, as so seldom they are aright, from above. On the further cliff, the woodland mantle parts broadly here and there to display great bays of rhododendron. They are chiefly the common *R. ponticum*, a plant with which familiarity has bred something stronger than contempt; but viewed from afar in this way nothing could be more beautiful than those great pools and channels of soft rose interrupting the surrounding verdure.

The beauty of this garden is greatly enhanced by its unison with the castle perched above it, which, originally built by the Dalzell, Earl of Carnwath, was sold in 1647 to James Hamilton, second son of John of Orbiston, who built wings to the old keep. Too many similar houses either have been abandoned for more commodious mansions and been suffered to moulder in dishonoured neglect, or have been unskilfully and inharmoniously enlarged to meet the requirements of modern households. Dalzell Castle has escaped both these indignities. The original keep, grimly and massively defensive, with walls seven feet thick, received large additions in the picturesque style of the seventeenth century. Imminent was the danger of disfigurement when it was determined to make it yet larger in the mid-Victorian era—an affluent period which was so fatal to many a historic pile; but the late Lord Hamilton was gifted with a nice judgment in matters structural and decorative, and also had the rare advantage of co-operation with R. W. Billings, who, for three whole years, devoted his rare knowledge and skill to enlarging and beautifying the old house, leaving it so that neither antiquaries, aesthetes, nor landscape gardeners can find foothold for a single unkind comment.

The castle occupies a site close to the Roman

military road, known as Watling Street, and antiquaries may hear, with less or more scepticism, that
the garden summer-house was built in 1736 on the
site of a Roman camp. The spacious grounds beyond
and around the terraces are planted with many choice
trees and flowering shrubs. Never have I seen such
abundance of pink and crimson hawthorn—pity 'tis
that the lord of this fair demesne should miss them
in their prime, for, like the Laird o' Cockpen,

"His mind it ta'en up wi' affairs o' the State"

at this season.

Midway between the house and the kitchen garden
is a well-ordered rose garden, sheltered from cutting
winds by thriving conifers, deciduous trees, and
hybrid rhododendrons. Two very shapely scarlet
oaks add much grace to this part of the grounds.
A dell near the carriage drive has been planned as
a bog garden on a scale exceeding the means of
keeping rampant growth in restraint. Coarse herbs
almost invariably get the upper hand in such places
to the obliteration of lowlier plants, and I saw little
to enjoy here except bamboos, Siberian iris, and
double lady's smock. It is a place to suit *Primula
japonica*, which, when first brought to this country
in 1874 was priced at 30s. a piece, but can now be
grown in profusion by scattering the seed in moist
places. The original strong crimson of this flower,
dangerously near magenta, has broken into a variety
of charming tints of pink, cream, and lavender.

BARNCLUITH

ARNCLUITH, or Baron's Cleugh as it used to be, and should be still called, is in the same densely-peopled, clangorous, tram-ridden, smoke-shaded district as Dalzell, lying scarcely outside the mining and manufacturing town of Hamilton, as Dalzell does outside Motherwell. But the seclusion of one is as perfect as that of the other, owing to the precipitous nature of the glen where it is built and the luxuriant greenwood which clothes the cliffs on each side of the Avon. Like Dalzell also in this, that it owes its erection to a Hamilton, namely, John of Broomhill, ancestor of the present Lord Belhaven, who built the triple dwelling house in 1583. Dorothy Wordsworth dismissed it in a sentence, devoting pages to describe the oppressive splendour of Hamilton Palace on the other side of the high road; but it is certain that neither she nor her husband can have penetrated this delectable pleasaunce, for no poet might view unmoved such a felicitous fusion of art with nature. In good truth the approaches to

186

BARNCLUITH.

BARNCLUITH

Barncluith are the reverse of promising. You turn off the tram line to the east of the town, and follow for half a mile or so what was once a country lane, but is now a partly-built line of small villas or large cottage dwellings. Great trees have been uprooted to make way for these, the roadway is worn into deep ruts in the course of transition into a common street, along which you proceed until, with dramatic suddenness, the scene changes. The way parts in two, passing on either side of a row of the weirdest sycamores you ever saw. Stretching their immense arms across both roads, these half dozen venerable giants remind one of the fantastic growths in Salvator Rosa's impossible forests. The right-hand road leads up to the gateway which admits to Hamilton High Parks, where the wild white cattle still browse beneath the gnarled oaks of Cadzow Forest; the one to the left descends to another gate, within which round a narrow plateau of closely-mown sward, stand at different elevations the three houses which form the mansion of Barncluith. One is puzzled to understand why there should be three, instead of but one, nor have I met anybody who could explain the mystery; howbeit, the resulting effect is picturesque in the highest degree.

"Barncluith," says Mr. Neil Munro, "is of all the ancient dwellings in that romantic neighbourhood the one which should most bewitch the angler; it was so obviously built for peace and an artistic eye and the propinquity of good fishing, while all the others were built for war."

SCOTTISH GARDENS

But you will hasten forward to view the garden—not that modern arrangement of parterres which occupies the further end of the plateau, which, indeed, is bright enough with roses and summer flowers within a girdling yew hedge, fantastically carved according to the archaic craft of toxidendry, but that other garden to the west of the house where the ground falls sheer to the sparkling Avon two hundred feet below, whereof Mr. R. S. Lorimer has written—

"Barncluith is quite unlike anything else : a detailed description can convey but little idea of its charm. It is the most romantic little garden in Scotland. Lying on one side of a great wooded valley, it is a veritable hanging garden. Four or five terraces, one above the other, sticking on the side of a cliff the general angle of which is about 55 degrees. Two little summer houses, great trees of scented box, and the flowers gathered here you feel sure would be, not a bouquet, but a posy —such an atmosphere about the place. In the twilight or the moonlight destinies might be determined in this garden."

The risk would not be less, methinks, at high noon, for there are alleys here and shaded bowers where Sol at his meridian can never do more than temper the green gloaming. It is not a garden wherein children could be turned loose to play, for the terraces are narrow—little more than dizzy ledges—with no guardian rail or breastwork to break or prevent a fall. The great extent of buttressed walls, with narrow borders at the foot, offer the most fascinating field for the enthusiast in horticulture. At present ivy runs riot over far too much of the wall-space, which might be occupied by an extensive collection of the choicest flowering shrubs. The borders also, effectively as they are stored with familiar things, such as rockets, stocks, poppies, wall-flower and ferns, present the most tempting variety of aspects to meet the requirements of every kind of hardy subject. This most enviable demesne has lately passed into the hands of a new owner (or at least occupier) for whom a most absorbing occupation lies await, if he has any turn for it, in improving these terraces into one of the most remarkable gardens in existence, horticulturally, as it is already architecturally.

For the rest, these terraces are a fantasia of clipped yew and box. One need not grudge the labour spent on this somewhat barbarous form of decoration, albeit one may prefer a tree in the form which God has prescribed for it to one hewn laboriously into the shape of a peacock or a tea-pot. Nevertheless, there is time and money spent here upon what one cannot but regard as misdirected industry. For instance, the whole length of one of these terraces is occupied by no less than forty little square beds in the Dutch manner, each with its box edging, each enclosed with a gravel path. Weeding these paths and clipping this box must absorb a considerable amount of attention, without a corresponding spectacular result ; for the effect would be far finer were these toy beds thrown into one long border, filled with the flowers of all seasons. They are designed, of course, for the separate cultivation of masterpieces of the florist's skill, and, if employed in that way, would form a distinct and attractive feature ; but devoted as they are merely for the display of common flowers, the effect is meaningless and irritating.

The delights of this garden are greatly enhanced by the lovely views up and down the winding Avon, and across to the rich woodland on the further shore. And over all reigns that sense of seclusion and repose which cannot fail to appeal to the hard-wrought man of affairs as strongly as to the habitual loiterer.

DUNROBIN

UNROBIN CASTLE occupies on the east coast a position similar to that of Culzean Castle on the west. Each is built on the summit of a high sea cliff, the broad Moray Firth stretches in front of one as the spacious Firth of Clyde does before the other; and each has been in possession of the same family from a time anterior to any written record. We find, at least, no documentary evidence of the ownership of Dunrobin previous to 1197, when the territory of Sutherland was forfeited by Harold Maddadson, Norse Earl of Caithness, for rebellion, and bestowed by William the Lion upon Hugh, son of Freskin the Fleming. From this Hugh the present Duke of Sutherland traces direct descent through his great-grandmother, Elizabeth, daughter and sole heir of the nineteenth Earl of Sutherland.

In yet another respect these two houses enjoy a common characteristic, inasmuch as the climate of Dunrobin is almost, if not quite, as favourable to the growth of choice and delicate vegetation as that of

191

SCOTTISH GARDENS

Culzean, although Dunrobin is 280 miles further north than Culzean, and the winter of inland Sutherland is far more severe than that of Ayrshire. It is difficult to account for the peculiar clemency which distinguishes the shores of the Moray Firth, for that great inlet lies far out of the direct course of the gulf stream; but certain it is that, wherever shelter can be provided from the furious winds which rage in this region during the winter months, all forms of vegetation display vigour and luxuriance in a remarkable degree. Robert Gordon of Straloch, geographer and cartographer to Charles I., took note of this.

"Dunrobin, the Erle of Sutherland his speciall residence, a house well seated upon a mote hard by the sea, with fair orchards, when ther be pleasant gardens planted with all kinds of froots, hearbs and floors [flowers] used in this kingdom, and abundance of good saphorn [saffron], tobacco and rosemarie, the froot being excellent, and cheeflie the pears and cherries."

One is disposed to murmur at the taste of an age which swept away this old garden and its contents, to make way for terraces and parterres on a grand scale in the Italian manner, when the second Duke of Sutherland enlarged the castle in 1845-51; nevertheless, the ground lies so beautifully, the views from the terrace stairs are so commanding, and the trees crowd down so close to the tide, that the whole effect is very fine. At all events, we have here an example, scarcely to be surpassed elsewhere, of the art of horticulture as it prevailed in the early Victorian era. Should the passion for cultivating rare plants ever

DUNROBIN.

overtake a lord of this stately demesne, soil, aspect and climate combine to assure him of an ample reward.

In the garden of Dunrobin one cannot but be impressed, as in other historic Scottish houses, with a sense of contrast between past and present. Where everything seems so orderly and secure, it is good to remember the system of anarchy and violence which once over-rode all law. No part of Scotland was more fiercely riven with blood-feuds than the counties of Sutherland and Caithness. Administration of justice was, of necessity, committed to the barons, and, like all hereditary functions, was liable to gross abuse when it passed into unworthy hands.

The chronicle of crime and terrorism in these counties is so confused, the actors in deeds of violence changed sides so often, that it is difficult to follow the intricate narrative. But in the sixteenth century two implacable rivals stand out among the ruck of minor marauders in the persons of the Earl of Sutherland and the Earl of Caithness. In 1514 the Earldom of Sutherland devolved upon Elizabeth, sister of John, eleventh earl. She married Adam Gordon, second son of the Earl of Huntly, and her husband became titular Earl of Sutherland. Adam, being a man of common sense, determined to put an end to the wasteful rivalry between the house of Dunrobin and the Earl of Caithness. Each had a common enemy in the clan Mackay, inveterate brigands, who raided the lands of both earls with fine impartiality. Adam made over certain lands in Strathullie, now known as Helmsdale, to the Earl of Caithness, in consideration for assistance to be given against the Mackays. Caithness took possession of the lands, and straightway joined forces with the Mackays, who, during Sutherland's absence in Edinburgh, made a destructive raid upon the lands of Dunrobin. The countess was at home, however, and sent out her natural brother, Alexander Sutherland, who overtook the Mackays at Torran-dubh, near Rogart, and inflicted upon them a bloody defeat. "This," wrote Gordon of Straloch, "was the greatest conflict that hitherto hes been foughtin between the inhabitants of these countreyes, or within the diocy of Catteynes, to our knowledge."

Alexander might have lived prosperous and popular after this, but his victory over the Mackays turned his head. He made alliance with the hereditary enemies of his house, marrying the sister of the very chieftain whom he had overthrown at Torran-dubh, and laid claim to the earldom of Sutherland, alleging that he was no bastard, but had been born in wedlock. He had a considerable following in the Sutherland clan, and, assisted by the Mackays, seized Dunrobin Castle when the Earl was again absent. The earl returned, however, raised his clan, recaptured the castle in which Alexander had left a garrison, and, in a subsequent raid by Alexander, took that gentleman, struck off his head and stuck it on a pole on the top of Dunrobin Castle, " which shews us," says Gordon of Straloch, " that whatsoever by fate is allotted, though sometimes foreshewed, can never be avoyded. For the witches had told Alexander the bastard that his head should be the highest that ever wes of the Sutherlands; which he did foolishlye interpret that some day he would be earl of Sutherland, and in honour above all his predecessors."

For more than fifty years after this the two earls and their successors waged almost incessant guerrilla upon each other's lands and people, a condition of affairs far from unusual between country neighbours in Scotland during that troubled century, but accompanied in this instance by deeds of more than common brutality. When Queen Mary came to the throne, John Gordon, twelfth Earl of Sutherland, known as " Good Earl John," held the upper hand; but he was forfeited and banished in 1563 on a charge of complicity in the rebellion of his kinsman, the Earl of Huntly. After Queen Mary's abdication in 1567, he was restored by Act of Parliament, and returned to Sutherland with his third wife, widow of the fourth Earl of Menteith.

During Sutherland's exile, you may be sure that the Earl of Caithness had not been idle. He had induced Sutherland's uncle, Gilbert Gordon of Gartay, to marry Isobel Sinclair of Dunbeath. Gilbert died, leaving one son, John, who lived with his mother at Helmsdale Castle, a lonely fortalice about thirteen miles north eastward along the coast from Dunrobin.

Sutherland, also, had but one son, Alexander, who alone stood between Isobel's son and succession to the earldom. Caithness persuaded his kinswoman Isobel that Alexander must be put out of the way. What will not woman dare and do for the sake of her son? But more was wanted. A single murder would not suffice, for the Countess of Sutherland was known to be near her confinement. Caithness insisted that a clean sweep must be made of the whole brood.

This was planned in the following way. In July, 1567, Isobel invited the Earl and Countess of Sutherland, with their son, Lord Alexander, to spend a few days at Helmsdale, that the young lord might enjoy some sport with the deer in Strathullie. One evening she put poison in the ale prepared for supper. Sutherland and his countess drank of it, and were taken ill; but Lord Alexander remained late on the hill and supper was finished before he and John Gordon, Isobel's son, returned. Sutherland, feeling the poison at work and suspecting the truth, dragged off the table-cloth, forbade his son to take bite or sup in that house of death, and sent him forward fasting to Skibo. The Earl and Countess managed to get to Dunrobin, where they both died within five days; but not before their death had been avenged by a strange stroke of fate. Isobel, probably, had made some pretext to keep her son out of the supper-room; but the lad, being thirsty and tired with hunting, sent a servant for a horn of ale, which he quaffed, fell ill, and died after two days of agony. The wretched mother was taken by Sutherland's people, sent to Edinburgh for trial, was condemned to death, and only escaped execution by taking her own life in prison, after denouncing the Earl of Caithness as having commanded her to commit the crime.

The said Earl was by no means diverted from his purpose by the miscarriage of his plot. The new Earl of Sutherland being under age, John Earl of Atholl was appointed his guardian, who most nefariously sold the wardship to Caithness himself, Sutherland's deadliest enemy, who carried the young earl off to the grim fortress of Girnigo, scene of innumerable and unspeakable cruelties. Even in that secret retreat, however, he did not dare immediately to attempt the life of his ward. As a preliminary, perhaps, he compelled him to marry his daughter, Lady Barbara Sinclair, a woman of open profligacy, the paramour of Mackay of Far. The bride was two-and-thirty ; the bridegroom only fifteen. Caithness then took up his abode at Dunrobin, where he destroyed all the Sutherland papers, and proceeded to administer his son-in-law's estates, inaugurating a reign of terror, the memory whereof still haunts the hills and shores of this fair land. Many he drove from their homes by violence, slaying those who resisted and forcing others by inhuman tortures to surrender their property. He did not spare even his own son, the Master of

Caithness, who displeased him by showing too
much mercy to the people of Dornoch, whom he
had been ordered to massacre. He kept him in a
dungeon at Girnigo for seven years, at the end of
which the wretched man was put to a horrible
death. His gaolers were two cousins of his own,
David and Ingram Sinclair. Whether they wearied
of their duty, or whether Caithness instructed them
now to bring it to an end, certain it is that they
left their prisoner without food for two or three
days, then supplied him liberally with salt beef,
gave him nothing to drink and left him to perish
in an agony of thirst.

The monster who could thus inhumanly treat
his own son and heir was not likely to show much
tenderness to him whom he had forced to become
his son-in-law. Nor did he so. In 1569 Caithness
left Dunrobin for Edinburgh, having given minute
instructions for the assassination of the young Earl of
Sutherland. The plot was betrayed to one of the
Gordons, who collected a party and concealed them in
Dunrobin Glen, not far from the castle. Alexander
Gordon of Sidderay then went forward, disguised as a
pedlar, obtained speech with Sutherland, warned him
of his danger, and bade him come to the glen next
morning. The servants of Caithness had instructions
never to let Sutherland out of their sight ; but
the young man managed to lead them to the
appointed place, where they sprung the ambush.
The Gordons overpowered the keepers, cut their

throats, and carried off their chieftain to the strong castle of Strathbogie.

Thereafter Sutherland managed to keep free from the clutches of his dangerous neighbour. Not only so, but he had no difficulty in obtaining decree of divorce against his wife, Barbara Sinclair, and in 1573 married Lady Jean Gordon, daughter of the fourth Earl of Huntly, the beautiful woman whom Bothwell had divorced in order to marry Mary Queen of Scots.

Standing on the terrace above the garden at Dunrobin, one is on the very scene of these and many similar deeds which seem well-nigh incredible in our humdrum age. The keep still stands wherein the tyrant Earl of Caithness kept Sutherland a prisoner doomed to death, for it is incorporated in the great pile erected by the second Duke of Sutherland. From the same standpoint may be seen a memorial of a later age—the age of Gargantuan conviviality—in the shape of a large garden-house below the castle. This now is fitted up as a museum, and contains a fine collection of local antiquities and natural history; but it served a different purpose in the eighteenth century. Hither the lord of the castle used to adjourn with his guests after an early dinner, to spend the long evening plying them with strong wine. Outside the servants assembled towards midnight on the broad stairway leading to this temple of Bacchus, the duty of each being to recover his master and lead (or carry) him to bed.

SCOTTISH GARDENS

Thus "the old order changeth, yielding place to new." Each generation of men lives in a different fashion from the last; but the blackbird's note in Dunrobin Glen—the plover's pipe on Dunrobin shore—the scream of the eagle on Beinn Dobhrain—the yelp of the fox on Creag-a-ghlinne—have changed no whit since the Norsemen first drew up their black *kyuls* on Golspie strand.

Yet there is one sound which the people of these glens once had good reason to recognise with dread, that is no longer heard hereabouts—the howl of the grey wolf. It was at the very close of the seventeenth century that some sheep were destroyed in the Glen of Loth, about half way between Dunrobin and Helmsdale. At first this was believed to be the work of dogs, for it was supposed that the last of the wolves had been killed two or three years before in Assynt and Halladale. But an old hunter named Polson, living at Wester Helmsdale, recognising the real character of the culprits, set out with his son and a herd laddie to explore the recesses of Glen Loth. This is a place of many memories, for here, where the Sletdale burn joins the Loth, are the standing stones of Carrickachlich, Cairnbran, where Fingal's good dog Bran lies buried, and the holy well of Tobermassan. In the ravine of Sletdale Polson found his quest in the shape of a rift in the rocks, with the ground well trodden into a track leading into it. The fissure widened inwards, but was too narrow to admit a full-grown man; so, having first failed to rouse what inmates there might be by throwing in stones, the two lads were sent in to explore the cavern, while Polson kept watch outside. Sure enough, they found a litter of fine whelps, and shouted news of their discovery to Polson.

"Kill them quickly," he cried, poking his head into the crevice, "and come away."

Just as he withdrew his head, a great she wolf, which had come up unobserved, dashed past him into the hole. Luckily, he managed to catch and keep hold of her bushy tail, which he twisted round his left arm; but it required the force of both arms to hold the maddened brute; Polson dared not loose his right hand to draw his knife, and his gun was out of reach. His son, all unaware of the mortal struggle outside, cried out from inside—

"It is dark here now, father; what is stopping the light from us?"

"You'll soon know," answered Polson, "if the root of the tail was to break!"

After this had gone on for some time, the wolf lay still for a moment or two to gather strength; Polson made a snatch for his knife, and stabbed the animal in the hind-quarters, which made her turn and attempt to come out of the hole. But the hunter had the powerful beast at a disadvantage; keeping her jammed between the rocks, he managed to plant his blade in a vital part, and the last wolf in Sutherland shed its life-blood on the rocks and heather.

STOBHALL

N one respect the beautiful house of Stobhall impresses one with melancholy. It
is a notable and commendable example
of the manner in which ancient architecture should be preserved from the
ravages of our most edacious climate ; but it is no
longer "a home," except for the caretaker, whose
presence only seems to accentuate the silence which
reigns undisputed where of old—

> "Joy was within and joy without,
> Vnder that wlonkest waw [splendid wall],
> Quhair Tay run down with stremis stout
> Full strecht vnder Stobschaw."

The lands of Stobhall were granted by Robert the
Bruce to Sir Malcolm Drummond after the great
victory of Bannockburn, when so many of English
Edward's barons were dispossessed of their estates
in Scotland. It was the birthplace of Sir Malcolm's
great-granddaughter, Annabella, who became Queen
of Scots by her marriage with Robert III. It has
descended through a long line of Drummonds to its

STOBHALL.

present owner, the Earl of Ancaster, whose abode is in Strathearn, at Drummond Castle, famous for its architectural garden and terraces. Some might deem that garden more worthy than Stobhall of a place in this series, but it has been made the subject of so many essays and illustrations that we have given preference to the lonely and less well-known house in Strathtay.

In truth, there is little that can be called a garden at Stobhall, only the place once bright with summer flowers, whereof a few, such as the grey asters in Miss Wilson's picture, have clung to the soil, marking the change of seasons as the old sundial does the fleeting hours, till hours and seasons together roll up into centuries. Perhaps the place is fairer in its desolation than it ever was when it teemed with busy life. Certes, it would be difficult to find in all Scotland a more enchanting scene than I beheld one May morning on visiting this spot. The pearl-grey walls of the old house gleamed softly in the sunshine, deeply mantled in the fresh verdure of sycamore and beech. Steeply sloped the greensward to the river, starred and wreathed with late narcissus, purple orchis, and myriad humbler blooms. Far below where I stood, the Tay, lordliest of Scottish rivers, swept in smooth curves, shimmering in the light, glowering in the shade, to fling itself in sudden tumult over the Linn o' Campsie. And all around, far as the eye could range, was wealth of woodland, ancient trees and affluent tillage.

SCOTTISH GARDENS

What a paradise of flowers might be created here! which, after all, is but a sorry pretext for including among Scottish gardens a place where a garden was, but is not. Our excuse is that Stobhall remains in its desolation one of the most fascinating places in the realm.

Those who are curious in architecture will find in the buildings interest that they miss in the garden. As at Barncluith, instead of a single mansion there is a group of detached dwellings, the oldest and chief of them bearing the date 1578, and containing a remarkable chapel and rooms for priests. The ceiling of the chapel is in five compartments, each painted with figures on horseback, except one, which represents Rex Mauritanæ mounted on an elephant. This decoration, coupled with the profusion of heraldic devices and the repetition Drummond motto GANG WARILY, recalls the coloured roofs of the Château de Blois, with the everlasting salamander of François I^{r.} One cannot be too grateful to the family which has so faithfully preserved this choice example of the Scottish renaissance.

RAEDEN HOUSE

OBERT, by the grace of God King of Scots, in the course of the strenuous years when he was making good his claim to that exalted title (being as yet recognised by the Pope and King Edward of England only as the rebel Robert de Brus, sometime Earl of Carrick), did receive no little encouragement and support from the burgesses of Aberdeen; whereof he made due note at the time. Certain monarchs have been known to do the like under similar stress of circumstances, yet have they failed to consult their tablets after the fortune of war has put it in their power to recompense such services. But Robert the Bruce had ever a warm heart and a liberal hand. Moreover, the expulsion of English landowners furnished him with ample means for rewarding his adherents; wherefore, when the King had come to his own, the royal burgh of Bon Accord was among the first to receive substantial recognition of help rendered in time of need. Upon the burgesses and community was conferred a royal charter, confirming them in possession of their burgh and infefting them, their heirs and successors for ever, as owners of the royal forest of the Stocket, saving only to the Crown the timber growing in the said forest and such beasts of the chase as might chance to be found therein.

Were good "King Hobbe" (as Edward Long-shanks used in derision to nickname his doughty opponent), permitted to revisit Aberdeen, it would be fine to watch his puzzled countenance as his eyes roved in vain quest for some familiar landmark. All, all is changed; only the river runs in its accus-tomed course. As for the forest, so earnestly have the Aberdonians exercised the right conferred in their charter of erecting "dwelling-houses and other buildings," that one can but guess now where were its precincts. Streets and terraces climb the braes where of old the stag couched and the red fox prowled, a state of things whereof the memory lingers in the name of Mr. Barclay's pretty resi-dence, Raeden House—the lair of the roe. It was once the property of Provost More, who built himself here a country residence towards the end of the eighteenth century, and enclosed with high walls of lasting granite, faced with brick, an ample garden. House and garden are now sundered, the latter being occupied by a market-gardener; and Mr. Barclay has filched from his pasture land the flowerbeds which Miss Wilson has depicted in their autumn glow of chrysanthemums. It is a charmingly tran-

RAEDEN HOUSE.

quil retreat, for although the tide of villas has flowed around it, and continues to flow, fine old trees confer a venerable appearance upon the mansion, and completely screen it in sequestered dignity from the world of trams and pillar boxes outside.

It would be difficult to contrive a climatic contrast more rapid and complete than I experienced in leaving London on a dripping, smoke-laden evening in June, and arriving next morning in brilliant sunshine at Aberdeen. The all-prevailing granite of the northern city (Aberdeen possesses the only granite-built cathedral in the world) sparkled clear and clean-cut in the morning rays ; neither streets nor houses bore any suggestion of the grime and mud engrained upon those of London, and the drive out to Raeden lay through suburbs wreathed in verdure and garden fronts gay with *Clematis montana*, laburnum, hawthorn red and white, lilacs, *Weigelia* and hybrid rhododendrons. True, there was a "snell" north wind ; but nothing could dim the brightness or stint the abundance of blossom on tree and shrub and herb.

COCKER'S NURSERY

ASSING from Raeden House over the hill-top known as the Cocket Hat, one comes upon a wide extent of nursery ground; and, forasmuch as our series of Scottish garden types would not be complete without a sample of commercial horticulture, Miss Wilson has chosen a corner of this ground called Honey Braes, which forms a fitting subject for her art. The day may come when this drawing may have an interest more than æsthetic; for already this part of the nurseries has been marked off in building plots, and the red-roofed house is doomed to disappear at no distant date. It was under these red tiles that Mrs. Byron (*née* Catherine Gordon of Gight) lived with her son George, whom she described to her sister-in-law, Mrs. Leigh, as being "very well and really a charming boy" in 1791. Seven years later the "charming boy" succeeded his great-uncle, the "wicked Lord Byron," as sixth Lord Byron, with such results upon English literature as we wot of. It suggests curious commentary upon early training and what surprises may await those who calculate upon its result, to read Byron's notes upon his start in letters. "I had," he says, "a very serious, saturnine, but kind young man, named Paterson, for my tutor. He was the son of my shoemaker, but a good scholar, as is common with the Scotch. He was a rigid Presbyterian also."

The owner of this nursery, Mr. James Cocker, is an enthusiast in his profession, one in whose company an eager amateur will find no summer's day too long. Field by field the speculative builder has encroached upon his border, and field by field he has retreated further into the country. Roses are his speciality; but there is much else to interest him who concerns himself, like the present writer, more with natural species than with florists' varieties. The first display to attract attention on this bracing June morning was a breadth of St. Bernard's lily—the fine variety known as *Anthericum liliago majus* or *Algeriense*. Myriads of milk-white, golden-anthered blossoms of perfect shape waved in the breeze, suggesting irresistibly the question—why is this lovely lily so seldom seen in private gardens? The answer may be supposed to be that its flowering season coincides with the summer meetings at Epsom and Ascot, when so many country people of means and leisure, however little they may care personally for racing, leave the country at its fairest to undergo the rush and discomfort of a London season.

The Chilian *Ourisia coccinea*, so chary of its brilliant

flowers in most gardens, was thickly set with scarlet tubes in an open, but rather shady, border. Alpine anemones, both the white and the sulphur, were just over, but bore traces of recent display in hundreds of seed-tufts on tall stems. Very conspicuous and attractive was a seedling perennial lupine, bearing spikes of clear salmon colour, and near it a starry firmament of globe-flowers (*Trollius*), lemon-yellow, sulphur and fiery orange, none of them, in our opinion, equal in grace and delicacy to the native *T. europœus*.

Pansies and violas were in infinite variety and copious bloom, the pure tints of these easiest of flowers being admirably shown up by the plan of planting them in strips of different colours drawn diagonally across a long border. *Incarvillea grandiflora*, hitherto reputed somewhat tender, here grows in the open and on the flat as generously as its taller and better known relative *I. Delavayi*; and that, as we all have learnt to our content, combines the constitution of a dandelion with the refinement of a gloxinia.

Sisyrinchium odoratissimum I have not seen elsewhere. It is to be hoped that Mr. Cocker will succeed in propagating it, for it is an interesting thing, hanging out white bells striped with purple on airy stalks a foot and a half high. The rarest treasure in the herbaceous section is a pure white *Alstrœmeria chilensis*, of which Mr. Cocker possesses a single plant, obtained, after long and difficult negotiation, from an amateur who raised it.

A pretty feature in these nurseries is a pergola

flowers in most gardens, was thickly set with scarlet
tubes in an open, but rather shady, border. Alpine
anemones, both the white and the sulphur, were just
over, but bore traces of recent display in hundreds
of seed-tufts on tall stems. Very conspicuous and
effective was a seedling perennial lupine, bearing
spikes of clear salmon colour, and near it a starry
tuft of globe-flowers (*Trollius*), lemon-yellow,
passing very orange, none of them, in our opinion,
equal in grace and delicacy to the native *T. europœus*.

Pansies and violas were in infinite variety and
copious bloom, the pure tints of these easiest of flowers
being admirably shown up by the plan of planting
them in strips of different colours drawn diagonally
across a long border. *Incarvillea grandiflora*, hitherto
reputed somewhat tender, here grows in the open and
flowers as generously as its taller and better known
relative *I. Delavayi*; and that, as we all have learnt
to our cost, combines the constitution of a dandelion with the refinement of a gloxinia.

Rhododendron odoratissimum I have not seen elsewhere, and it is to be hoped that Mr. Cocker will succeed
in propagating it, for it is an interesting thing,
bearing white bells striped with purple on airy
stems a foot and a half high. The rarest treasure in
the herbaceous section is a pure white *Alstrœmeria
chilensis*, of which Mr. Cocker possesses a single plant,
obtained, after long and difficult negotiation, from an
amateur who raised it.

A pretty feature in these nurseries is a pergola

COCKER'S NURSERY, ABERDEEN.

of laburnum, which only requires to be mixed with *Wistaria* to create a perfect summer dream. But as *Wistaria* flowers uncertainly and sparingly thus far north, this design might be carried out effectively in warmer districts. An interesting example of the influence of scion upon stock may be seen in this pergola. Laburnum with variegated leaves having been grafted upon the ordinary species at a height of five feet or so, the stock has responded by putting out variegated leaves at a considerable distance below the graft.

SMEATON-HEPBURN[1]

HADDINGTONSHIRE

MEATON-HEPBURN is delightfully situated on the river Tyne in the most fertile champaign of all Scotland—the seaward portion of the county of Haddington. The remarkable collection of trees, shrubs, and flowering herbs which adorns the grounds owes it affluence to the enthusiasm of two generations of amateurs, for to the love of trees which inspired the late Sir Thomas Buchan-Hepburn, his son and successor Sir Archibald has added a keen intelligence in the cultivation of herbaceous and alpine plants. The herbaceous plants occupy borders in the old-fashioned walled garden; where also is a teeming and interesting nursery of that most perplexing, yet fascinating race, the Saxifrages. *S. Elizabethæ* and *apiculata* are particularly luxuriant, having overflowed in verdant volume the stone compartments assigned to

[1] Owing to a severe illness in the spring of 1908, Miss Wilson unfortunately was prevented from visiting Smeaton-Hepburn in order to make a drawing in the garden there. Notwithstanding the consequent absence of a plate, I have thought that a few notes about this fine collection of shrubs and plants may be not without interest.

them. Two kinds of wind-flower, *Anemone alpina* and *palmata alba* were in great beauty when I saw these borders last; and at that time, the end of May, the most conspicuous wall shrubs were *Ceanothus rigidus* sheeted with deep blue, and *Coronilla emerus*, *pointillé or*, as heralds would term it—in plain language sprinkled with clear canary yellow. Both these last betoken a genial, sunny climate, albeit we are here a long way north on the east coast.

For the alpines, Sir Archibald has prepared a home worthy of his treasures; a wide space sheltered by woods from cutting winds, yet lying fair to the sun, having been covered with rock-work constructed with far more attention to cultural requirements than to scenic effect. Here is no tea-gardenish attempt to mimic the Himalayas or ape the Andes; the plants are grouped upon raised ledges and mounds for the double purpose of securing rapid drainage and of bringing them under the eye for closer inspection; while rocks are employed, not for mere effect, but to check radiation and evaporation, which, in excess, are the two chief adversaries to plant growth, and to provide a cool and natural root run for exacting mountaineers. To do justice to this fine collection would have taken more hours than I had to spare. Among the species which their luxuriance made it impossible to overlook were *Gentiana verna*, that capricious beauty so seldom seen taking kindly to imprisonment; *Mitella trifida*, more attractive than the rest of the genus; *Saxifraga rhei superba*, really justifying its additional epithet,

213

Primula farinosa making a miniature grove of rosy bloom, *Ramondia pyrenaica* and *Nathaliæ*, flowering profusely, but inclined to gasp for cooler shade. Prostrate phloxes, *Arenaria* and encrusted saxifrages peopled the slopes in lavish abundance. The charming Chatham Islands sorrel, *Oxalis enneaphylla*, had just opened one or two of its milky blossoms, and the time of *Dianthus* and *Campanulæ* was at hand when a fresh chord of colour would be struck.

Near the mansion house a fine deodar, 70 or 80 years old, stands in sisterly proximity to *Cupressus macrocarpa* from the opposite hemisphere. They have been of mutual benefit to each other by encouraging upward growth, and so preventing that podgy, lateral spread which is so destructive of the true character of most conifers. When will landscape gardeners learn that fine park timber cannot be had without submitting it first to forest discipline?

A splendid bush of *Garrya ellyptica* stands on the lawn before the house. It measures 63 feet in circumference, and is the growth of 47 years, for it was killed to the ground in the winter of 1861.

In crossing the park to the lake, one cannot fail to be charmed by the clouds of poet's narcissus springing from the turf in all directions. Never have I seen such a display; they have run abroad in millions. Perhaps there is no other flower which unites purity of colour so completely with simple grace of form. Was this, think you, the species whereof Mahomet spoke when he said—"Let him who hath two loaves sell one, and buy flower of narcissus; for bread is but food for the body, whereas narcissus is food for the soul"?

The most delectable part of all this demesne lies round the lake. A precipitous crag screens the southern shore, planted with many choice trees and shrubs. It is a great pleasure to be escorted thither by Mr. Brown, who has tended these grounds for more than fifty years, and can show you conifers 100 feet high planted by himself under direction of the late Sir Thomas Hepburn. Specially notable are *Picea sitchensis* and *Abies nobilis,* and by ascending to the summit of the crag you may have the pleasure, unusual in this country, of viewing these lofty trees from a level with their tops. Here and there advantage has been taken of clearings in this fine wood to plant Himalayan rhododendrons, bamboos and other shelter-loving growths.

ENVOI

Farewell dear flowers: sweetly your time ye spent,
Fit while ye lived for smell or ornament,
      And after death for cures.
I follow straight, without complaints or grief,
Since, if my scent be good, I care not if
      It be as short as yours.

George Herbert.

APPENDIX A

MENTION may be made of a few species of rhododendron which have been proved to endure the climate of the West of Scotland as far north as Ross-shire. Partial shade overhead is beneficial, and they must be completely sheltered from violent winds. It is best to start them in a compost of peat and coarse sand in equal parts; afterwards they will thrive in any free or light soil provided it does not contain lime in any form. The flowers of the early kinds may be destroyed by frost in some seasons, but their beauty is so great as to compensate for many failures by success in a favourable year; and the foliage of most species is so decorative that the plants deserve cultivation for that alone. What is most to be dreaded is frost in April or May, after growth has begun. This too often destroys the terminal shoots and buds, but their place will be taken by the secondary ones. As most of these rhododendrons are costly, it will be prudent to proceed tentatively at first with a few of the hardiest species, which are marked in the following list by an asterisk (*), and to give them every possible advantage of shelter from wind.

[The above was written before the destructive frost of 24th April 1908, which caught early rhododendrons in full growth and destroyed masses of bloom. Probably it has also ruined the prospects of next year's blossom, for the secondary growths are feeble and bear few flower buds.]

Species.	Colour of Flower.	Height.	Time of Flowering.	Remarks.
Rhododendron Aucklandi,	Pearl white -	8-10 ft.	v	Leaves 10-15 in. long. Flowers very large. There are fine pink and crimson varieties. Sikkim.
* ,, arboreum, -	White, rose or blood red	15-20 ft.	iii-v	Beautiful waxy flowers. Sikkim.

APPENDIX A

Species.	Colour of Flower.	Height.	Time of Flowering.	Remarks.
*Rhododendron barbatum, -	Intense blood red	40-50 ft.	iii, iv	One of the hardiest. There is a rose coloured variety. Sikkim.
* ,, calophyllum,	White - -	3-5 ft.	v	Sikkim. Flowers tubular.
* ,, campanulatum,	Pale lilac -	8 ft.	iv	Very hardy. Sikkim.
* ,, Campbelli, -	White, with crimson spots	20-30 ft.	iv, v	Sikkim.
* ,, campylocarpum,	Sulphur or clear yellow	6 ft.	iv	Sikkim.
* ,, Caucasicum, -	Rosy outside white within	1 ft. spreading	vii	The Caucasus.
* ,, ciliatum, -	Reddish purple or white	2 ft. spreading	v	Sikkim. Very hardy and fragrant. One of the best.
* ,, cinnabarinum,	Orange-red and yellow	10 ft.	v, vi	Sikkim. Long, tubular flowers, something like *Fuchsia conica.* Being late in bloom it escapes spring frosts.
* ,, cinnamomeum,	White, spotted purple	15-20 ft.	iv	Of *arboreum* type.
* ,, decorum, -	—	—	—	A newly introduced Japanese species, which I have not yet seen in flower; but the foliage is magnificent and it appears quite hardy.
,, Edgworthi, -	Pure white -	3 ft. straggling	v, vi	Sikkim. Very large flowers.
* ,, Eximium, -	Cream, with purple base	—	vi	Bhotan. Very fine foliage, nearly akin to *R. Falconeri.*

218

APPENDIX A

Species.	Colour of Flower.	Height.	Time of Flowering.	Remarks.
*Rhododendron Exoniense, -	White, tinged rose	5 ft.	v	Sikkim. Very fragrant.
* ,, Falconeri, -	White - -	30 ft.	v	Sikkim. One of the hardiest, but impatient of wind. Should be well mulched in the manure or brewers' draff to encourage the splendid foliage.
* ,, ferrugineum, -	Bright rose -	2 ft.	v-vii	The Alpine Rose: Central Europe.
* ,, Fordii, - -	White - -	—	vi	China.
* ,, Fortunei, -	Pale pink -	12 ft.	v	China. Very hardy, with large flowers. Parent of many hybrids.
* ,, fulgens, - -	Blood red -	6 ft.	iv, v	Eastern Himalayas.
* ,, glaucum, -	Apple blossom rose	6 ft.	v	Sikkim. Leaves aromatic.
,, grande, - -	White - -	30 ft.	iii, iv	Sikkim. Known also as R. argenteum. One of the finest, but somewhat tender and a shy flowerer.
* ,, hirsutum, -	Bright rose -	2 ft.	v-vii	Alpine Rose, very near R. ferrugineum, but better.
* ,, Hodgsoni, -	Pale purple or rose	20 ft.	v, vi	Eastern Himalayas. Grand foliage.
* ,, Keysi, - -	Red and yellow	6 ft.	vii	Bhotan. Resembles R. cinnabarinum.

APPENDIX A

Species.	Colour of Flower.	Height.	Time of Flowering.	Remarks.
Rhododendron lacteum,	White - -	—	vi	China. Hardy in Wicklow. Immense leaves.
* ,, *lanatum,* -	Primrose dotted red	15 ft.	vi	Sikkim.
,, *Maddeni,* -	White - -	8 ft.	vi, vii	Sikkim.
* ,, *maximum,* -	Pale rose dotted yellow, red or brown	20 ft.	vii	North America. Named *maximum* before Sir J. Hooker discovered the more lofty Sikkim species.
* ,, *Niveum,* -	Dark lilac -	15-20 ft.	v	Sikkim. Fine foliage: very hardy.
* ,, *parvifolium,* -	Pale rose -	2-3 ft.	iv, v	China. Quite hardy.
* ,, *racemosum,* -	Pale pink -	Dwarf	iv, v	Western China. Quite hardy.
* ,, *Rhodora,* -	Rosy - -	4 ft.	iii	North America. Quite hardy: deciduous.
* ,, *Roylei,* -	Purplish red -	8 ft.	v, vi	Sikkim.
* ,, *Smirnowi,* -	Rose - -	6 ft.	iv, v	Caucasus. Quite hardy. Fine foliage.
* ,, *Thomsoni,* -	Blood red -	10 ft.	v, vi	Sikkim. One of the best.
,, *Wighti,* -	Yellow, spotted crimson	12 ft.	vi	Sikkim.

APPENDIX A

OF the common hybrid rhododendrons it is not necessary to give a selection : everyone may choose for himself at the annual shows. Many of them are marvellous productions, but even the best of them are deficient in the appearance of *race* which distinguishes the natural species. They are wanting, also, in the subtle harmony between flower and foliage which is such a fine feature in the wild rhododendrons. But these defects are not present in the following hybrids which are scarcely, if at all, inferior in these respects to the true species.

Species.	Colour of Flower.	Height.	Time of Flowering.	Remarks.
Rhododendron *Altaclarense,* -	Bright red ·	20 ft.	iv	*R. catawbiense* × *ponticum.*
„ Ascot Brilliant,	Scarlet · ·	—	v	—
„ *Beauty of Tremough,*	Rose · ·	—	—	Raised by Mr. Gill, Tremough, Cornwall.
„ *Broughtoni,* -	Deep rose ·	20 ft.	v, vi	An *arboreum* hybrid. Immense truss and fine foliage.
„ George Hardy,	Rose · ·	15 ft.	v, vi	—
„ Gill's Triumph,	Rose · ·	—	iv, v	A lovely flower, larger than Pink Pearl, but not so hardy.
„ Gloria Penjerrick,	Rose · ·	—	iv, v	Do., do.
„ *Harrisi,* ·	Deep rose ·	—	iii	*R. arboreum* × *Thomsoni.*

APPENDIX A

Remarks.	Colour of Flower.	Height.	Time of Flowering.	Species.
Rhododendron Kewense, -	Rose - -	12 ft.	iv, v	*R. Aucklandi* × *Hookeri.*
„ *Luscombei,* -	Rose - -	—	iv	*R. Fortunei* × *Thomsoni.*
„ *Manglesi,* -	White, purple spotted	—	—	*R. Aucklandi* × *album elegans.*
„ Mrs. Stirling,	Blush - -	—	v, vi	—
„ *Nobleanum,* -	Carmine, pale pink or white	16 ft.	i-iv	*R. arboreum* × *caucasicum.*
„ Pink Pearl, -	Rose - -	—	vi	Of *Aucklandi* type. Raised originally by the late Peter Lawson of Edinburgh.
„ *præcox,* - -	Mauve - -	8 ft.	ii, iii	*R. ciliatum* × *dauricum.*
„ Sappho, -	White, with dark, almost black, throat	—	v, vi	A very showy variety.
„ *Shilsoni,* -	Bright crimson	12 ft.	iv	*R. barbatum* × *Thomsoni.*
„ *Smithianum,* -	Yellow - -	—	vi	A very fine variety.

APPENDIX B

THE following is a list, far from exhaustive, of shrubs, other than rhododendrons, reputed more or less tender in the London and Midland districts, which have proved quite hardy in many parts of Scotland, especially in the West. Discretion should be exercised in the time and mode of planting. It is not advisable to plant such things in the open between the end of August and the beginning of May. Protection should be given during the first winter by a circle of wire netting loosely filled with dry bracken. Rough wind is far more to be dreaded than cold. Those species of which I have not personal experience are marked †.

Name.	Colour.	Height.	Season of Flower.	Remarks.
Abelia floribunda, -	Rose purple -	3 ft.	iv	*Caprifoliaceæ.* A Mexican shrub. Requires a wall in most districts.
Acacia dealbata, -	Yellow - -	20 ft.	iii, iv	*Mimoseæ.* Requires protection till established and shelter from wind at all times. Was killed to the ground by April frost in 1908 after growing 16 ft. high.
Akebia quinata, -	Dark brownish purple	10 ft.	v, vi	*Berberideæ.* A climber: China: flowers fragrant.
Aralia Sieboldii (Fatsia japonica),	White - -	10 ft.	viii	*Araliæ.* Stands moderate shade.
Azara microphylla, -	Yellow - -	18 ft.	ii, iii	*Bixineæ.* Very fragrant.

APPENDIX B

Name.	Colour.	Height.	Season of Flower.	Remarks.
Berberidopsis corallina,	Carmine - -	12 ft.	vi-viii	*Berberideæ.* From Chili. Requires wall.
Buddleia Colvillei, -	Rose - -	8 ft.	vi, vii	Sikkim. Has flowered freely in the open border at Edinburgh Botanic Gardens.
,, *globosa,* -	Orange - -	15 ft.	v-vi	*Loganacia.* From Chili.
,, *variabilis magnifica,*	Purple - -	15 ft.	vi, viii	China. A very superior variety of the species.
Callistemon coccinea, -	Carmine - -	5 ft.	v, vi	The bottle brush plant. Hardy in the S.W. Flowers annually on a wall with the protection of a mat in winter.
Camellia japonica, -	Red, rose or white	12 ft.	iv, v	*Ternstræmiaceæ.* Best on a wall, sheltered from wind.
Carpenteria californica,	White, yellow centres	10 ft.	vi, vii	*Saxifragaceæ.* Flowers freely on a wall as far north as Invernesshire.
Chionanthus virginicus,	White - -	15 ft.	vi, vii	*Oleaceæ.* "The Fringe Tree." Perfectly hardy as a standard in the west.
Choysia ternata, -	White - -	10 ft.	v, vi	*Rutaceæ.* From Mexico. Stands any amount of frost in the open, if sheltered from cutting winds.
Clethra acuminata, -	White - -	10-15 ft.	viii-x	*Ericaceæ.* Carolina.
,, *alnifolia,* -	White - -	4-5 ft.	viii-x	N. America. Both species are very fragrant, *C. acuminata* being the better one.

APPENDIX B

Name.	Colour.	Height.	Season of Flower.	Remarks.
Clianthus puniceus, -	Rosy scarlet -	Climber	v	*Papilionaceæ.* On a south wall.
Cordyline australis, -	White - -	20 ft.	v, vi	*Liliaceæ.* Individual plants vary much in hardiness. The old leaves should not be cut off.
Coronilla glauca, -	Yellow - -	4-5 ft.	vi-ix	*Papilionaceæ.* Quite hardy in E. Lothian.
Desfontainea spinosa, -	Scarlet and yellow	4-5 ft.	vii-viii	*Loganaciæ.* Like so many Chilian plants, this revels in the humid atmosphere of the west, but was severely cut by spring frost in 1908.
Eccremocarpus scaber,	Reddish orange	Climber	vi-viii	*Bignonaceæ.* Chili.
† *Embothrium coccineum,*	Scarlet - -	20 ft.	vi	*Proteaceæ.* I have not seen this fine shrub flowering in Scotland; but as it succeeds splendidly in Ireland it ought to do so on the west coast.
Erica arborea, - -	Rose or white -	10 ft.	iv, v	—
„ *lusitanica,* -	White - -	10 ft.	iv, v	*Ericaceæ.*
Escallonia exoniensis, -	White - -	15 ft.	vii, viii	—
„ *macrantha,*	Rose - -	15 ft.	vi, vii	*Saxifrageæ.* Chili. The Escallonias are perfectly hardy in the west of Scotland. Perhaps the handsomest is *E. Langleyense,* a hybrid.

APPENDIX B

Name.	Colour.	Height.	Season of Flower.	Remarks.
Escallonia rubra, -	Red - -	15 ft.	vii	
Eucryphia cordifolia, -	White, flushed rose	20 ft.	viii, ix	*Eucryphiaceæ*. Chili. This and the following species, which succumb to the winter at Kew, have resisted 22 degrees of frost in my garden.
„ *pinnatifolia*, -	White - -	15 ft.	vii, viii	—
Fabiana imbricata, -	White - -	3-4 ft.	v	*Solanaceæ*. Chili. I have failed to keep this curious shrub, but have seen it growing luxuriantly 350 feet above the sea in Ayrshire.
Fuchsia globosa, -	Crimson and purple	15 ft.	vi-ix	*Onagraceæ*. Mexico. This species and its offspring *Ricartoni* are the hardiest; but many other species succeed on a brick wall, or in an open border as herbaceous growth. Among the best are *F. conica* and *serrulata*.
Garrya ellyptica, -	Grey-green catkins	12 ft.	xii, i, ii	*Cornaceæ*. California. Requires a wall in cold districts: but grows freely in the open in E. Lothian.
Hydrangea hortensia, -	White, blue or rose	3-4 ft.	viii, ix	*Saxifragaceæ*. China. All species of Hydrangea luxuriate near the sea, sheltered from the blast.

226

APPENDIX B

Name.	Colour.	Height.	Season of Flower.	Remarks.
Illicium religiosum, -	Ivory - -	4 ft.	iv, v	*Magnoliaceæ.* Japan. Uninjured by 22 degrees of frost in 1907.
Indigofera Gerardiana,	Rose - -	5 ft.	viii, ix	*Papilionaceæ.* Himalayas.
Mutisia decurrens, -	Bright orange	Climber	vi, vii	*Compositæ.* A brilliant climber, quite hardy, east and west. Chili.
Myrtus communis, -	White - -	10 ft.	viii, ix	*Myrtaceæ.* S. Europe. Except at sea level on the west coast myrtle requires the shelter of a wall.
,, (*Eugenia*) *apiculata,*	White - -	10 ft.	vii, viii	Quite hardy in the open.
Nandina domestica, -	White - -	5-6 ft.	viii, ix	*Berberidaceæ.* Pretty foliage, taking fine autumnal tints. China.
Notospartium Carmichaliæ,	Rosy lilac	20 ft.	vii, viii	*Papilonaceæ.* New Zealand.
Olearia Haasti, -	White - -	10 ft.	viii, ix	*Compositæ.* New Zealand. There are numerous species all desirable, especially *O. Gunni, macrodonta, nitida, nummularifolia* and *insignis.* Except *O. Haasti,* these and the following species are liable to be killed to the ground in inland districts.
Oxydendron (*Andromeda*) *arborea,*	White - -	40 ft.	vi, vii	*Ericaceæ.* Besides its fine blossoms this plant takes vivid autumnal tints.

APPENDIX B

Name.	Colour.	Height.	Season of Flower.	Remarks.
Ozothamnus rosmarinifolius,	White - -	10 ft.	vii, viii	*Compositæ.* Australasia.
Parrotia persica, -	Crimson stamens, no petals	10 ft.	ii	*Hamamelideæ.* Central Asia. Grows freely as a standard without suffering from frost, but I have not seen it flower. Fine autumn foliage.
Pieris (Andromeda) formosa,	White - -	6 ft.	vi, vii	*Ericaceæ.*
Piptanthus nepalensis,-	Yellow - -	10 ft.	v	*Papilionaceæ.* Nepaul. In the west does not require a wall.
Rhus cotinoides, -	Reddish -	20 ft.	vi, vii	*Anacardiaceæ.* Splendid leaf colour in autumn. North America.
Sophora (Edwardsia) tetraptera,	Yellow - -	8 ft.	v	*Papilionaceæ.* New Zealand. Flowers best on a sunny wall.
Trachycarpus (Chamærops) excelsus,	Yellow - -	20 ft.	v, vi	*Palmæ.* A perfectly hardy palm, only requiring shelter from wind. The old leaves should not be cut off.
Tricuspidaria lanceolata,	Crimson - -	10 ft.	iv	—
Vaccinium corymbosum,	Rosy white -	10 ft.	v, vi	*Vacciniaceæ.* Beautiful alike in flower and foliage. North America.
Zenobia (Andromeda) speciosa pulverulenta,	Pearly - -	4 ft.	vi, vii	*Ericaceæ.* Thrives best among decaying logs.

APPENDIX C

DECORATIVE shrubs, herbs, and bulbs, suitable for an all-British border. Although the plants in this list are all truly indigenous to the United Kingdom, some of them are so local in distribution or have become so rare that they must be obtained through the trade. Such plants are marked with an asterisk (*). The months of flowering are indicated by Roman numerals.

RANUNCULUS FAMILY. *Ranunculaceæ.*

English Names.	Botanical Name.	Colour.	Height.	Time of Flowering	Remarks.
Alpine Meadow Rue	*Thalictrum alpinum*	Purplish	6 in.	vii, viii	Requires peat. Foliage pretty, like *Adiantum.*
Lesser Meadow Rue	*Thalictrum minus*	Yellowish or pale purple	1-4 ft.	vi, vii	Foliage resembling maidenhair, and more durable in water.
Meadow Rue Fen Rue }	*Thalictrum flavum*	Yellow	2-4 ft.	vii, viii	Likes a moist soil.
Pasque Flower	*Anemone pulsatilla*	Purple	6-12 in.	v, vi	Deep soil, with chalk or lime.
Wood Anemone Wind Flower }	*Anemone nemorosa*	White, with rosy and lavender varieties	4-8 in.	iv, v	The most beautiful variety is called *Robinsoniana,* of a charming lavender hue with gold stamens.
Rose-a-ruby Red Morocco Pheasant's Eye Red Maidweed }	*Adonis autumnalis*	Scarlet with dark spot	1 ft.	v-ix	An annual; requires a sunny exposure.
GreaterSpearwort	*Ranunculus lingua*	Bright yellow	3 ft.	vii-ix	A very handsome buttercup for waterside or moist border.

APPENDIX C

English Names.	Botanical Name.	Colour.	Height.	Time of Flowering	Remarks.
Buttercup Crowfoot St. Antony's Rape	*Ranunculus bulbosus* fl. pl.	Bright yellow	1 ft.	vi-ix	Only the double flowered forms of this and the following species are admissible.
Buttercup Crowfoot Crazy Gold Knots	*Ranunculus acris* fl. pl.	Bright yellow	1-2 ft.	vi-ix	
Marsh Marigold King Cups Brave Bassinets Boots Meadow Bouts Mare Blobs	*Caltha palustris*	Bright yellow	1 ft.	iii-vi	There are double flowering forms, *nana plena* and *monstrosa plena*. For waterside or moist border.
Globe Flower Troll Flower Lucken Gowan	*Trollius europœus*	Clear, pale yellow	1-2 ft.	vi-viii	Better than any exotic species. Likes a moist border.
Bear's Foot Oxheel Setterwort	*Helleborus fœtidus*	Pale green	4 ft.	i-iii	Fine bold foliage, a good winter plant. Likes lime
*Columbine Culverwort	*Aquilegia vulgaris*	Blue	1-3 ft.	v-vii	There are many varieties, single and double, of various colours.
Larkspur Knight's Spurs	*Delphinium ajacis*	Bright blue	1-1½ ft.	vi, vii	An annual, with pink and white varieties.
*Monkshood Wolfsbane Friar's Cap Aconite	*Aconitum napellus*	Dark blue	2-3 ft.	vi	Easily naturalised in open woods.
Baneberry Herb Christopher	*Actœa spicata*	White	1-2 ft.	v, vi	Has black, poisonous berries, whence the name Baneberry.
*Pæony	*Pæonia officinalis*	Crimson	1-3 ft.	v, vi	Only found on Steep Holme Island in the Severn, whence it has been nearly extirpated.

230

APPENDIX C

BARBERRY FAMILY. *Berberideæ.*

English Names.	Botanical Name.	Colour.	Height.	Time of Flowering	Remarks.
Barberry Pipperidge }	*Berberis vulgaris*	Pale yellow	16 ft.	v	There are 43 varieties enumerated in the Kew hand list.

WATERLILY FAMILY. *Nymphæaceæ.*

English Names.	Botanical Name.	Colour.	Height.	Time of Flowering	Remarks.
Water Lily	*Nymphæa alba*	White	Floating	v-viii	
Yellow Water Lily Brandy-bottle Candock }	*Nuphar luteum*	Yellow	Floating	vi-viii	Would be more highly esteemed if we had not the white water lily.

POPPY FAMILY. *Papaveraceæ.*

English Names.	Botanical Name.	Colour.	Height.	Time of Flowering	Remarks.
Corn Poppy Cop Rose Headwarke Joan Silverpin Cheese Bouts }	*Papaver rhœas*	Scarlet.	1-1½ ft.	vi-viii	There are many varieties and sports of this native poppy, the most beautiful being those known as "Shirley" poppies.
Longheaded Poppy	*Papaver dubium*	Scarlet	1 ft.	vi-viii	Very near the last species.
Rough Poppy	*Papaver hybridum*	Red	1½ ft.	vi-viii	Requires poor soil: chalk.
Pale Poppy	*Papaver argemone*	Pale red	6 in.-1 ft.	vi-viii	All our true poppies are annuals.
Welsh Poppy	*Meconopsis cambrica*	Yellow	1-2 ft.	v-ix	There is a double variety, and a beautiful orange one, this and a variety of the next species being the only instance of this colour in British wild flowers. This plant is a true perennial.

231

APPENDIX C

English Names.	Botanical Name.	Colour.	Height.	Time of Flowering	Remarks.
Horn Poppy	*Glaucium luteum*	Clear yellow	2-3 ft	vi-viii	A biennial. Plant in pure sand and grit. There is a beautiful orange variety with a dark spot.

FUMITARY FAMILY. Fumariaceæ.

Yellow Corydal	*Corydalis lutea*	Yellow	1 ft.	v-viii	Good on old walls.

WALLFLOWER FAMILY. Cruciferæ.

Stock Stock-gilliflower	*Matthiola incana*	Violet	1-2 ft.	v-viii	The parent of the Brompton and Queen Stocks.
Wallflower Chevisaunce Wild Cheir	*Cheiranthus cheiri*	Yellow to red	1-1½ ft.	ii-v	Parent of innumerable varieties.
Winter Cress	*Barbarea vulgaris* fl. pl.	Yellow	1-2 ft.	vi-ix	The double flowered variety is showy.
Lady's Smock Cuckoo Flower Spinks	*Cardamine pratensis* fl. pl.	Pale lilac	1 ft.	iv, v	The double variety is worth a place in a moist border.
Sweet Alison	*Alyssum maritimum*	White	4-10 in.	vi-ix	Valuable for its fragrance.
Whitlow Grass	*Draba azoides*	Bright yellow	2, 3 in.	iii	A pretty alpine.
Candytuft	*Iberis amara*	White	6-9 in.	vi, vii	An annual.

ROCK ROSE FAMILY. Cistineæ.

Spotted Rock Rose	*Helianthemum guttatum*	Yellow, with red spot	6-12 in.	vi-viii	An annual.
Rock Rose	*Helianthemum vulgare*	Clear yellow	3-10 in.	v-viii	Parent of the garden rock-roses, single, double, and of many colours.

APPENDIX C

VIOLET FAMILY. *Violaceæ.*

English Names.	Botanical Name.	Colour.	Height.	Time of Flowering	Remarks.
Violet	*Viola odorata*	Violet, white, or intermediate	3-5 in.	iii-v	
Dog Violet	*Viola canina*	Lavender, bluish lilac, or white	3-5 in.	iii-v	Makes a beautiful mass of colour when grown by itself in rather poor soil.
Pansy Herb Trinity Heartsease Love-in-idleness Kiss Me Fancy Flamy Three Faces under a Hood	*Viola tricolor*	Purple, blue, white, yellow or mixed	3-9 in.	v-ix	All the show and fancy varieties of Pansy can be claimed as derived from this British wildflower.

PINK FAMILY. *Caryophyllaceæ.*

*Maiden Pink	*Dianthus deltoides*	Bright rose or white	6-9 in.	vi-ix	
*Cheddar Pink	*Dianthus cæsius*	Pink	3-6 in.	vi, vii	Lime and sand.
Soapwort Bouncing Bet Bruise-wort Fuller's Herb	*Saponaria officinalis*	Lilac or white	1-2 ft.	viii, ix	There is a double variety.
*Cushion Pink Moss Campion	*Silene acaulis*	Rose, crimson or white	2 in.	vi, vii	For the rock or wall garden.
Bladder Campion Spatling Poppy Witches' Thimble	*Silene inflata*	White	6 in.-1 ft.	vi-viii	The glaucous maritime form is the best.
Nottingham Catchfly	*Silene nutans*	White or pink	2-3 ft.	v-vii	
Night Catchfly	*Silene noctiflora*	Rose inside, yellow outside	1-2 ft.	vi, vii	Flowers at night: fragrant.

2 F

233

APPENDIX C

English Names.	Botanical Name.	Colour.	Height.	Time of Flowering	Remarks.
White Campion	*Lychnis vespertina*	White	1-3 ft.	v, viii	
Rose Campion	*Lychnis diurna*	Rose	1-3 ft.	iv, ix	The double form is best.
Ragged Robin	*Lychnis flos-cuculi*	Rose	1-2 ft.	v, vi	
*German Catchfly	*Lychnis viscaria*	Red-purple	10-18 in.	vi	There are several varieties, including a double one.
*Alpine Catchfly	*Lychnis alpina*	Rose	4-6 in.	vi	
Vernal Sandwort	*Arenaria verna*	White	1-3 in.	vi	
Sea Purslane	*Arenaria peploides*	White	3-4 in.	v-viii	For wall, garden, or rockwork
Fringed Sand-wort	*Arenaria ciliata*	White	2-3 in.	vi, vii	
Alpine Chick-weed	*Cerastium alpinum*	White	2-4 in.	vi, vii	

TAMARISK FAMILY. *Tamariscineæ.*

English Names.	Botanical Name.	Colour.	Height.	Time of Flowering	Remarks.
Tamarisk	*Tamarix gallica*	Pink	6-12 ft.	vii-ix	Evergreen shrub.

ST. JOHN'S WORT FAMILY. *Hypericineæ.*

English Names.	Botanical Name.	Colour.	Height.	Time of Flowering	Remarks.
Tutsan, Park Leaves, Sweet Amber	*Hypericum androsæmum*	Yellow	2-3 ft.	vi-viii	
St. John's Wort	*Hypericum perforatum*	Yellow	2-3 ft.	vii-ix	

234

APPENDIX C

FLAX FAMILY. *Linaceæ.*

English Names.	Botanical Name.	Colour.	Height.	Time of Flowering	Remarks.
Pale Flax	*Linum angustifolium*	Pale blue	1-2 ft.	v-ix	} Perennials.
Perennial Flax	*Linum perenne*	Bright blue, pink or white	12-18 in.	vi, vii	
Flax Line	} *Linum usitatissimum*	Blue	1½ ft.	vi, vii	An annual.

MALLOW FAMILY. *Malvaceæ.*

Marsh Mallow Hock Herb	} *Althæa officinalis*	Blush	3-4 ft.	vi, vii	Moist soil.
Musk Mallow	*Malva moschata*	Rose or white	2-3 ft.	vii, viii	
Tree Mallow Velvet Leaf	} *Lavatera arborea*	Purple	6-10 ft.	viii-x	

GERANIUM FAMILY. *Geraniaceæ.*

Bloody Cranes-bill	*Geranium sanguineum*	Crimson	1 ft.	vi, vii	The rose-coloured variety *lancastri-ense* is best.
Meadow Cranes-bill	*Geranium pratense*	Violet blue	2-3 ft.	vi, vii	There are white and double blue varieties.
Wood Cranesbill	*Geranium sylvestre*	Violet blue	2 ft.	vi, vii	There is a white variety.

SPINDLE FAMILY. *Celastrineæ.*

Spindle Tree Prick-wood Gad-rise Louse-berry	} *Euonymus europæus*	Green	5-20 ft.	v	Valuable for its beautiful rose-coloured berries. There is a variety with white berries.

APPENDIX C

LEGUMINOUS FAMILY. *Leguminosæ.*

English Names.	Botanical Name.	Colour.	Height.	Time of Flowering	Remarks.
Furze Whin Gorse }	*Ulex europæus*	Yellow	3-10 ft.	iv, v	There is a fine double-flowered variety.
Dwarf Furze	*Ulex nanus*	Yellow	2-3 ft.	viii-x	
Greenweed	*Genista pilosa*	Yellow	Prostrate	v, vi	
Dyer's Greenweed Woodwaxen Base Broom }	*Genista tinctoria*	Yellow	1-2 ft.	vii-ix	
Broom	*Cytisus scoparius*	Yellow	5-8 ft.	v, vi	There are many varieties, including *Andreanus*, with reddish-brown standard.
Lucern Sickle Medick Snail's Horn }	*Medicago falcata*	Pale yellow or violet	Prostrate	vi, vii	
Clover	*Trifolium incarnatum*	Crimson	9-12 in.	vi, vii	An annual.
Birdsfoot Trefoil Butterjags Crow-toes }	*Lotus corniculatus*	Yellow	Prostrate	v-ix	Makes a fine display on wall garden. There is a double-flowered variety.
Woundwort Kidney Vetch Lambs' Toe }	*Anthyllis vulneraria*	Yellow, white, pink or red	6-18 in.	vi-viii	A fine variety, *Dilleni*, has cream-coloured flowers with red tips.
Purple Milk-vetch	*Astragalus hypoglottis*	Purple	3 in.	v, vi	There is a white flowered variety.
*Alpine Milk-vetch	*Astragalus alpinus*	Purple	Prostrate	vi	There is a white flowered variety.
Sweet Milk-vetch	*Astragalus glyciphyllus*	Sulphur	Prostrate	vi	
*Mountain Vetch	*Oxytropis campestris*	White and purple	3-6 in.	vii	

APPENDIX C

English Names.	Botanical Name.	Colour.	Height.	Time of Flowering	Remarks.
* Purple Mountain Vetch	*Oxytropis uralensis*	Purple	3-6 in.	vi, vii	
Sainfoin French Grass Cock's Comb }	*Onobrychis sativa*	Bright rose	2-3 ft.	v, vi	
Tufted Vetch	*Vicia cracca*	Purple	Climber	vi-viii	
Wood Vetch	*Vicia sylvatica*	White and blue	Climber	vi, vii	

ROSE FAMILY. *Rosaceæ.*

English Names.	Botanical Name.	Colour.	Height.	Time of Flowering	Remarks.
Dwarf Cherry Mazzards Merry }	*Prunus cerasus*	White	15-20 ft.	iv, v	There are many beautiful varieties, including a double white.
Wild Cherry Gean }	*Prunus avium*	White	20-60 ft.	iv, v	Do. do.
Birdcherry Hackberry }	*Prunus padus*	White	20-30 ft.	v	Many varieties, but none better than the type.
Willow Spiræa	*Spiræa salicifolia*	Pink	3-5 ft.	vii, viii	There are white and other varieties.
Meadow Sweet Queen of the Meadows Meadwort Bridewort }	*Spiræa ulmaria*	Cream	2-4 ft.	vi-viii	There is a double variety.
Dropwort	*Spiræa filipendula*	White	2-3 ft.	vi, vii	There is a fine double form.
Mountain Avens	*Dryas octopetala*	White	Prostrate	v, vi	Likes lime.
Cloudberry Noops }	*Rubus chamæmorus*	White	4-6 in.	vi, vii	Peat and sand: moist. Has sweet yellow fruit.
Blackberry Black Boyds Bumblekite Scaldberry }	*Rubus fruticosus*	White and pink	Trailer	vi-ix	The double white and double pink forms are very ornamental.

APPENDIX C

English Names.	Botanical Name.	Colour.	Height.	Time of Flowering	Remarks.
Knotberry	*Rubus saxatilis*	Dull white	10 in.	vi, vii	Only useful for rock-garden on account of its carmine fruit.
Silverweed Goose Tansy }	*Potentilla anserina*	Yellow	Creeping	vi-ix	Were it not such a common weed this would be reckoned a lovely plant.
* Shrubby Cinquefoil	*Potentilla fruticosa*	Yellow	2-3 ft.	vi-viii	
Rock Cinquefoil	*Potentilla rupestris*	White	1-2 ft.	vi-viii	
Burnet Rose Scots Rose }	*Rosa pimpinellifolia*	Cream or pink	1-3 ft.	v, vi	Many cultivated varieties.
Sweetbriar Eglantine }	*Rosa rubiginosa*	Bright rose	3-6 ft.	vi	} There are many varieties.
Dog Rose	*Rosa canina*	Rose, pink, or white	6-15 ft.	vi, vii	
Downy Rose	*Rosa villosa*	White or pale pink	6-15 ft.	vi, vii	
Field Rose	*Rosa arvensis*	White	Trailing	vi-viii	
*Cotoneaster	*Cotoneaster vulgaris*	White	3-4 ft	v, vi	Easily naturalised, but only found wild in Britain on Great Orme's Head.

EVENING PRIMROSE FAMILY. *Onagraceæ.*

English Names.	Botanical Name.	Colour.	Height.	Time of Flowering	Remarks.
Rose Bay French Willow Willow Herb }	*Epilobium angustifolium*	Deep rose	4-6 ft.	vii, viii	
Codlins & Cream	*Epilobium hirsutum*	Deep rose	4-6 ft.	vii, viii	
Evening Primrose	*Onothera biennis*	Pale yellow	2-4 ft.	vii-ix	Really an American herb, but now thoroughly established among our native flora. The variety *Lamarckiana* is the best.

APPENDIX C

LOOSESTRIFE FAMILY. *Lythraceæ.*

English Names.	Botanical Name.	Colour.	Height.	Time of Flowering	Remarks.
Purple Loosestrife	*Lythrum salicaria*	Reddish purple	2-5 ft.	vii, viii	The varieties *roseum* and *superbum* are very fine.

STONECROP FAMILY. *Crassulaceæ.*

English Names.	Botanical Name.	Colour.	Height.	Time of Flowering	Remarks.
Roseroot Midsummer Men	*Sedum rhodiola*	Dull yellow or purplish	6-8 in.	vi, vii	
Orpine Livelong	*Sedum telephium*	Rose	1-1½ ft.	vii-viii	The best varieties of this plant should be chosen.
Wall-pepper Bird's-bread Pricket Jack-of-the-buttery Stonecrop	*Sedum acre*	Bright yellow	2-3 in.	vi, vii	
White Stonecrop	*Sedum anglicum*	White and rose	2-3 in.	vi, vii	Absurdly called English stonecrop; though common in Ireland and west Scotland, it scarcely is found in England.
Thickleaved Stonecrop	*Sedum dasyphyllum*	White and rose	2-3 in.	vi, vii	
Worm grass	*Sedum album*	White	4-6 in.	vi, vii	There are several varieties.
Rock Stonecrop	*Sedum rupestre*	Yellow	6-10 in.	vi-viii	There are some good varieties.
Stonor Trip-madam	*Sedum reflexum*	Yellow	8-10 in.	vi-viii	
Houseleek Ayegreen Youbarb Jupiter's Beard Bullock's Eye	*Sempervivum tectorum*	Red or dull purple	9-12 in.	vi, vii	The variety *rusticum* has broad bluish leaves.

APPENDIX C

SAXIFRAGE FAMILY. *Saxifragaceæ.*

English Names.	Botanical Name.	Colour.	Height.	Time of Flowering	Remarks.
* Purple Thirlstane	*Saxifraga oppositifolia*	Bright reddish purple	6 in.	iii-v	There are several fine varieties, but it is a mistake to grow the white-flowered one.
Yellow Thirlstane	*Saxifraga aizoides*	Yellow	6 in.	vi, vii	In damp, gritty loam.
Marsh Thirlstane	*Saxifraga hirculus*	Yellow	6 in.	vii-viii	Moist ground.
Eve's Cushion Dovedale Moss	*Saxifraga hypnoides*	White	6-12 in.	v-vii	
* Tufted Thirlstane	*Saxifraga cæspitosa*	White	3 in.	v-viii	
Meadow Saxifrage First of May	*Saxifraga granulata*	White	6-12 in.	iv, v	The double form is very fine.
*Alpine Thirlstane	*Saxifraga nivalis*	White	3-6 in.	vii, viii	
London Pride None-so-pretty St. Patrick's Cabbage Prattling-Parnel	*Saxifraga umbrosa*	White, red spots	8-12 in.	vi	
Kidney Saxifrage	*Saxifraga geum*	White, red spots	8-12 in.	vi	Not so good as the last.
Grass of Parnassus	*Parnassia palustris*	White	10-12 in.	vi	In moist ground.

UMBELLATE FAMILY. *Umbelliferæ.*

English Names.	Botanical Name.	Colour.	Height.	Time of Flowering	Remarks.
Astrantia	*Astrantia major*	Pink	1-3 ft.	vi, vii	The variety with greyish-white flowers should be avoided.
Sea Holly	*Eryngium maritimum*	Light blue	1 ft.	vii-ix	Plant in pure sand.

APPENDIX C

IVY FAMILY. *Araliaceæ.*

English Names.	Botanical Name.	Colour.	Height.	Time of Flowering	Remarks.
Ivy	*Hedera helix*	Greenish yellow	Creeper	ix, x	Innumerable varieties.

MISTLETOE FAMILY. *Loranthaceæ.*

Mistletoe	*Viscum album*	Green	Parasite	iii-v	Grows freely in the north if sown on poplar, apple, or hawthorn.

CORNEL FAMILY. *Cornaceæ.*

Dwarf Cornel	*Cornus suecica*	Purple with white bracts	6 in.	vii	Bears fine scarlet fruit. Moist peat and grit.

HONEYSUCKLE FAMILY. *Caprifoliaceæ.*

Wayfaring Tree	*Viburnum lantana*	White	8-15 ft.	v, vi	
Guelder Rose Water Elder Snowball Tree	*Viburnum opulus*	White	6-15 ft.	vi	The sterile variety should be cultivated.
Woodbine Honeysuckle	*Lonicera periclymenum*	Red and yellow.	Climber	vi-viii	
*Linnæa	*Linnæa borealis*	Pale pink	Prostrate	vi, vii	Moist heat and sand, in partial shade.

MADDER FAMILY. *Rubiaceæ.*

Lady's Bedstraw Maid's Hair Petty Mugget Cheese Rennet	*Galium verum*	Yellow	1½ ft.	vi-ix	Not usually reckoned fit for gardens, but beautiful and fragrant in a wall.
Woodruff	*Asperula odorata*	White	6-12 in.	v-vi	
Squinancy Wort	*Asperula cynanchica*	White streaked with blue.	9-12 in.	v-vi	

APPENDIX C

VALERIAN FAMILY. *Valerianeæ.*

English Names.	Botanical Name.	Colour.	Height.	Time of Flowering	Remarks.
Red Valerian Pretty Betsy	*Centranthus ruber*	Red or white	2-3 ft.	vi-ix	
Cat's Valerian All Heal Setwal Herb Bennet	*Valeriana officinalis*	Pale pink or white	3 ft.	vi-viii	

TEASEL FAMILY. *Dipsaceæ.*

English Names.	Botanical Name.	Colour.	Height.	Time of Flowering	Remarks.
Bluecaps Devil's Bit Forbitten More Blue Scabious	*Scabiosa succisa*	Blue	1-2 ft.	vi-ix	

COMPOSITE FAMILY. *Compositæ.*

English Names.	Botanical Name.	Colour.	Height.	Time of Flowering	Remarks.
Hemp Agrimony	*Eupatorium cannabinum*	Reddish-purple	2-4 ft.	vii	
*Alpine Fleabane	*Erigeron alpinus*	Lilac, yellow centre	9-12 in.	vii, viii	
Mountain Cud-weed Cat's Ear	*Gnaphalium dioicum*	Pink	3-6 in.	vi	
Goldilocks	*Linosyris vulgaris*	Yellow	2 ft.	viii, ix	
Goldenrod	*Solidago virgaurea*	Yellow	1-2 ft.	vii-ix	There is a dwarf variety, *cambrica*.
Elecampane Elfdock Horse-heal Scab-wort	*Inula Helenium*	Yellow	3-4 ft.	vi, vii	
Daisy Bruisewort Herb Margaret	*Bellis perennis*	White, pink and crimson	4-5 in.	iii-xi	The numerous double forms are well known.
Oxeye Moonwort Maudlinwort	*Chrysanthemum leucanthemum*	White with yellow centre	2-3 ft.	vi-viii	

242

APPENDIX C

English Names.	Botanical Name.	Colour.	Height.	Time of Flowering	Remarks.
Corn Marigold Bigold Boodle Goldins Gools	*Chrysanthemum segetum*	Yellow	1½ ft.	vi-x	An annual.
Oxeye Camomile	*Anthemis tinctoria*	Yellow	2 ft.	vii, viii	There are some splendid varieties.
Sneezewort Goosetongue	*Achillea ptarmica*	White	1-2 ft.	vi-ix	There are fine double varieties.
Yarrow Milfoil	*Achillea millefolium*	White or rose	1-2 ft.	vi-ix	
Cotton Weed Sea Cudweed	*Diotis maritima*	Yellow	8-10 in.	viii, ix	
Tansy	*Tanacetum vulgare*	Yellow	2 ft.	vii, viii	The variety *crispum* has beautiful foliage.
Milk Thistle	*Carduus marianus*	Rose-purple	1-4 ft.	vii-ix	Annual or biennial.
Scots Thistle Cotton Thistle	*Onoperdon acanthium*	Rose-purple	4-8 ft.	vii-ix	
Cornflower Bluebottle	*Centaurea cyaneus*	Bright blue.	2-3 ft.	vi-ix	Annual or biennial. Inferior forms are rose and purple.

BELLFLOWER FAMILY. *Campanulaceæ.*

English Names.	Botanical Name.	Colour.	Height.	Time of Flowering	Remarks.
Sheep's Bit	*Jasione montana*	Blue	1-1½ ft.	vi-ix	Annual
Rampion	*Phyteuma orbiculare*	Blue	6-18 in.	vii, viii	
Spiked Rampion	*Phyteuma spicatum*	Blue, white, or cream	1-3 ft.	vii	
Clustered Bellflower	*Campanula glomerata*	Blue	1-2 ft.	vi, vii	
Giant Bellflower	*Campanula latifolia*	Blue or white	3-6 ft.	vii	Likes shade of woods.

2 G 2

APPENDIX C

English Names.	Botanical Name.	Colour.	Height.	Time of Flowering	Remarks.
Nettle - leaved Bellflower.	*Campanula trachelium*	Blue	2-3 ft.	vii	
Creeping Bell-flower	*Campanula rapunculoides*	Blue	2-4 ft.	vi, vii	
Ramps Coventry Rapes }	*Campanula rapunculus*	Blue or white	2-3 ft.	vii, viii	
Bluebell Harebell Lady's Thimble }	*Campanula rotundifolia*	Sky blue	1 ft.	vii-ix	There is a white variety and a dark blue one, *Hosti*.
Ivy Bellflower	*Campanula hederacea*	Pale blue	Creeping	vii, viii	Moist ground.

HEATH FAMILY. *Ericaceæ*.

Bogberry	*Vaccinium uliginosum*	Pink	Trailer	v	Moist peat.
Cowberry Brawlins Flowering Box }	*Vaccinium Vitis-Idæa*	Pink	Trailer	vi	
Strawberry Tree	*Arbutus unedo*	White	8-12 ft.	ix	
Cranberry	*Vaccinium oxycoccus*	Pink	Creeping	v	Moist peat.
*Black Bearberry	*Arctostaphylos alpina*	White	Prostrate	iv	
Bearberry Mealberry }	*Arctostaphylos uva-ursi*	Pink	Trailer	iv	
Moorwort Marsh Rosemary Holy Rose }	*Andromeda polifolia*	Pink	8-10 in.	v-viii	Usually recommended for bog, but grows well in ordinary peat border.
St. Daboec's Heath	*Menziesia polifolia*	Purple or white	1-2 ft.	vi-ix	
*Blue Menziesia	*Menziesia cærulea*	Bluish purple	6-8 in.	vi, vii	One of the rarest British plants.

244

English Names.	Botanical Name.	Colour.	Height.	Time of Flowering	Remarks.
Heather Ling Grigg }	*Erica vulgaris*	Rose or white	1-3 ft.	viii, ix	There are a vast number of varieties, including a double rose.
Bell Heath	*Erica cinerea*	Crimson	6-12 in.	vii-ix	Many good varieties.
Cross - leaved Heath	*Erica tetralix*	Rose	6-12 in.	vii-ix	Many good varieties.
*Dorset Heath	*Erica ciliaris*	Pale red	6-12 in.	vi-ix	
Mediterranean Heath	*Erica carnea*	Bright rose	6-8 in.	i-iv	Should be clipped after flowering. There are white and deep - rose varieties.
Cornish Heath	*Erica vagans*	Pink or white	2 ft.	vii-ix	
*Wintergreen	*Pyrola uniflora*	White	6 in.	vi-viii	
Wintergreen	*Pylora rotundifolia*	White	6-10 in.	vii-ix	
Wintergreen	*Pyrola media*	White	6-10 in.	vii-ix	
Yevering Bells	*Pyrola secunda*	White	4 in.	vii	
Wintergreen	*Pyrola minor*	White	6-10 in.	vii-ix	

PRIMROSE FAMILY. *Primulaceæ.*

a. Primrose b. Cowslip, Paigle, Herb Peter, Palsy-wort c. Oxlip, Poly-anthus }	*Primula veris*	Sulphur	3 5 in.	iv, v	The Cowslip and Oxlip may be reckoned as racial varieties of the common Primrose. The varieties, single and double, are innumerable.
Bird's Eye Mealy Primrose }	*Primula farinosa*	Rosy lilac	3-12 in.	vi	

APPENDIX C

English Names.	Botanical Name.	Colour.	Height.	Time of Flowering	Remarks.
Sowbread	*Cyclamen europæum*	Rose or white	3-4 in.	viii, ix	
Yellow Pimpernel	*Lysimachia nemorum*	Yellow	Trailing	v-vii	
Creeping Jenny Moneywort Herb Twopence	*Lysimachia nummularia*	Yellow	Trailing	vi-viii	
Marsh Loosestrife	*Lysimachia thyrsiflora*	Yellow	1-3 in.	v, vi	Moist soil.
Yellow Loosestrife	*Lysimachia vulgaris*	Yellow	2-4 in.	vii, viii	
Star Flower Chickweed Wintergreen	*Trientalis europæa*	White	4-8 in.	vi, vii	

PERIWINKLE FAMILY. *Apocynaceæ.*

English Names.	Botanical Name.	Colour.	Height.	Time of Flowering	Remarks.
Large Periwinkle	*Vinca major*	Blue	1-2 ft.	iv, v	There is a white variety.
Periwinkle	*Vinca minor*	Blue, white or red	Trailer	iii-v	

GENTIAN FAMILY. *Gentianaceæ.*

English Names.	Botanical Name.	Colour.	Height.	Time of Flowering	Remarks.
Centaury Earthgall Christ's Ladder	*Erythræa centaurium*	Bright pink	4-6 in.	v-ix	There are several varieties.
*Marsh Gentian Wind Flower	*Gentiana pneumonanthe*	Sky blue	1-2 ft.	viii, ix	Deep moist soil.
*Spring Gentian	*Gentiana verna*	Gentian blue	3 in.	iv, v	Likes lime.
Yellow Wort	*Chlora perfoliata*	Yellow	3-12 in.	vii	An annual.
Buckbean Marsh Trefoil	*Menyanthes trifoliata*	White, flushed pink	1 ft.	v, vi	One of the loveliest of British wild flowers. A full bog plant.
Marsh Flower	*Limnanthemum nymphæoides*	Yellow	Floating	vii, viii	

APPENDIX C

PHLOX FAMILY. *Polemoniaceæ.*

English Names.	Botanical Name.	Colour.	Height.	Time of Flowering	Remarks.
Jacob's Ladder Greek Valerian Charity	*Polemonium cœruleum*	Blue or white	1-3 ft.	vi, vii	

BINDWEED FAMILY. *Convolvulaceæ.*

English Names.	Botanical Name.	Colour.	Height.	Time of Flowering	Remarks.
Bearbind Hedge Bells Campanelle	*Convolvulus sepium*	White	Climber	vii-ix	
Bindweed Cornbind	*Convolvulus arvensis*	Rose or white	Climber	vii-ix	
Sea Bindweed Sea Bells	*Convolvulus soldanella*	Pale pink	Prostrate	vi-viii	Plant in pure deep sand.

BORAGE FAMILY. *Boragineæ.*

English Names.	Botanical Name.	Colour.	Height.	Time of Flowering	Remarks.
Viper's Bugloss	*Echium vulgare*	Bright blue	2-4 ft.	vi-viii	A biennial.
Purple Bugloss	*Echium violaceum*	Bluish purple	3-4 ft.	vi-viii	A biennial.
Lungwort Jerusalem Cowslip	*Pulmonaria officinalis*	Rose changing to blue	6-12 in.	iv-vi	Has several good varieties.
Oyster Plant	*Mertensia maritima*	Pink changing to sky blue	Prostrate	v, vi	In deep sand and grit.
Purple Gromwell	*Lithospermum purpureo-cœruleum.*	Bluish purple	Prostrate	vi	
Forget-me-not Scorpion Grass	*Myosotis palustris*	Sky blue	6-12 in.	vi-viii	The white variety should never be grown.
Wood Forget-me-not Mouse-Ear	*Myosotis silvatica*	Sky blue	1-1½ ft.	vi-viii	
Alkanet Bugloss	*Anchusa officinalis*	Gentian blue	2 ft.	vi, vii	A biennial.
Green Alkanet	*Anchusa sempervirens*	Gentian blue	1½-2 ft.	—	A perennial.

APPENDIX C

NIGHTSHADE FAMILY. *Solanaceæ.*

English Names.	Botanical Name.	Colour.	Height.	Time of Flowering	Remarks.
Henbane	*Hyoscyamus niger*	Dull yellow, veined purple	1-2 ft.	vi-vii	A poisonous annual.
Dwale Deadly Nightshade Belladonna	*Atropa belladonna*	Purplish blue	1 ft.	vi-vii	A poisonous perennial.

FOXGLOVE FAMILY. *Scrophularineæ.*

English Names	Botanical Name	Colour	Height	Time of Flowering	Remarks
Great Mullein Hag Taper Jupiter's Staff Velvet Dock	*Verbascum thapsus*	Primrose	3-4 ft.	vi-vii	Biennial. All the mulleins are best raised from seed.
Dark Mullein	*Verbascum nigrum*	Yellow with purple filaments	2-3 ft.	vi-x	Perennial. There is a white variety.
White Mullein	*Verbascum lychnitis*	Yellow with white filaments	3-4 ft.	vi-vii	Perennial.
Moth Mullein	*Verbascum blattaria*	Yellow with purple filaments	2-3 ft.	vi-ix	Biennial.
Hoary Mullein	*Verbascum pulverulentum*	Yellow with white filaments	3-4 ft.	vi-ix	Perennial. Found only in East Anglia.
Toadflax	*Linaria vulgaris*	Citron and orange	1-2 ft.	vii-x	The variety *peloria* is very curious and showy.
Ivy Toadflax Kenilworth Ivy Mother of Thousands	*Linaria cymbalaria*	Lilac and white	Trailer	v-ix	
Foxglove	*Digitalis purpurea*	Red, purple, spotted, or white	3-5 ft.	vii	A biennial. Seed of many beautiful varieties can be had.
Spiked Speedwell	*Veronica spicata*	Bright blue	6-18 in.	vii, viii	There is a pink variety.
Rock Speedwell	*Veronica saxatilis*	Bright blue	6-8 in.	vii, viii	

APPENDIX C

LAVENDER FAMILY. *Labiatæ.*

English Names.	Botanical Name.	Colour.	Height.	Time of Flowering	Remarks.
Thyme Pell-a-mountain Brotherwort	*Thymus serpyllum*	Rosy purple	Prostrate	vi-viii	There are many fine varieties.
Woundwort	*Stachys germanica*	Rosy purple	1-3 ft.	vii, viii	
Bugle	*Ajuga reptans*	Blue	4-6 in.	v-vii	Good in shade: worthless elsewhere.

THRIFT FAMILY. *Plumbagineæ.*

English Names.	Botanical Name.	Colour.	Height.	Time of Flowering	Remarks.
Thrift Sea Gilliflower	*Armeria vulgaris*	Pink	3-6 in.	v-vii	There are crimson and white varieties.

KNOTWEED FAMILY. *Polygonaceæ.*

English Names.	Botanical Name.	Colour.	Height.	Time of Flowering	Remarks.
Bistort, Snakeroot	*Polygonum bistorta*	White or pink	1-2 ft.	vi-ix	
Copse Knotweed	*Polygonum dumetorum*	White	Climber	vii, viii	

DAPHNE FAMILY. *Thymeliaceæ.*

English Names.	Botanical Name.	Colour.	Height.	Time of Flowering	Remarks.
* Mezereon	*Daphne Mezerium*	Pink, red or white	2-4 ft.	ii-iv	

CATKIN FAMILY. *Amentaceæ.*

English Names.	Botanical Name.	Colour.	Height.	Time of Flowering	Remarks.
Bog Myrtle Sweetgale Candleberry	*Myrica Gale*	Inconspicuous	2-3 ft.	v-vii	

SPURGE FAMILY. *Euphorbiaceæ.*

English Names.	Botanical Name.	Colour.	Height.	Time of Flowering	Remarks.
Box	*Buxus sempervirens*	Green	3-16 ft.	iv	

APPENDIX C

ARUM FAMILY. *Aroideæ.*

English Names.	Botanical Name.	Colour.	Height.	Time of Flowering	Remarks.
Cuckoopint Wake-robin Lords-and-Ladies }	*Arum maculatum*	Purplish and green	8-12 in.	iv	There is a white-veined variety. The scarlet berries are the showiest part of this plant.

WATER PLANTAIN FAMILY. *Alismaceæ.*

Flowering Rush	*Butomus umbellatus*	Rosy lilac	3-4 ft.	vi, vii	In a ditch or pond margin.
Arrowhead	*Sagittaria sagittifolia*	White	—	vii-ix	There is a double-flowered variety. An aquatic which can be grown in moist border if started in water.
Floating Plantain	*Alisma natans*	White and yellow	Floating	vii, viii	

ORCHID FAMILY. *Orchidaceæ.*

Marsh Orchis Salep }	*Orchis latifolia*	Purple	1-3 ft.	vi, vii	
Hand Orchis Spotted Orchis }	*Orchis maculata*	Purple, lilac or white	6-18 in.	v-vii	
Soldier Orchis	*Orchis militaris*	Lilac, spotted purple	1-2 ft.	v	
Pyramid Orchis	*Orchis pyramidalis*	Rose	1 ft.	v-vii	
Long Purples Stander-wort }	*Orchis mascula*	Purple	8-10 in.	v	
Sweet Orchis	*Orchis conopsea*	Deep rose	8-10 in.	vi, vii	
Butterfly Orchis	*Habenaria bifolia*	Greenish white to ivory	8-12 in.	vi, vii	

English Names.	Botanical Name.	Colour.	Height.	Time of Flowering	Remarks.
No English name	*Cephalanthera grandiflora*	Cream	1-1½ ft.	vi	
	Cephalanthera rubra	Pink	1-1½ ft.	vi, vii	
*Lady's Slipper	*Cypripedium calceolus*	Chocolate and yellow	1-1½ ft.	vi	All but extinct in Britain. Our finest native orchid.

FLAG FAMILY. *Irideæ.*

English Names.	Botanical Name.	Colour.	Height.	Time of Flowering	Remarks.
Yellow Iris Sword Flag Orris	*Iris pseudacorus*	Yellow	2-3 ft.	v-vii	
Gladdon Roast beef plant	*Iris fœtidissima*	Pale grey blue	2-3 ft.	v-vii	
*Corn Flag Sword Lily	*Gladiolus communis*	Rosy	1½-2 ft.	vi	There are various shades from purplish to white.
Spring Crocus	*Crocus vernus*	Deep violet	4-6 in.	ii, iii	Parent of many garden varieties.
Naked Crocus	*Crocus nudiflorus*	Violet	4-8 in.	ix, x	

DAFFODIL FAMILY. *Amaryllideæ.*

English Names.	Botanical Name.	Colour.	Height.	Time of Flowering	Remarks.
Daffodil Lent Lily Crow Bells	*Narcissus pseudo narcissus*	Yellow	1 ft.	iii, iv	There are many varieties, double and single.
Primrose Peerless	*Narcissus biflorus*	White, with pale yellow centre	1 ft.	v	
Snowdrop Fair Maids of February	*Galanthus nivalis*	White and green	6-9 in.	i, ii, iii	The double form should be rigorously excluded.
Summer Snowflake	*Leucoium æstivum*	White and green	1-1½ ft.	v.	

APPENDIX C

LILY FAMILY. *Liliaceæ.*

English Names.	Botanical Name.	Colour.	Height.	Time of Flowering	Remarks.
Solomon's Seal ⎫ David's Harp ⎭	*Polygonatum multiflorum*	Greenish white	2-3 ft.	v, vi	
Lily - of - the - Valley	*Convallaria majalis*	White	6-8 in.	v, vi	
*May Lily	*Smilacina bifolia*	White	4-8 in.	v, vi	
Butcher's Broom ⎫ Box Holly Pettigrew ⎭	*Ruscus aculeatus*	Whitish	2-3 ft.	ii-iv	
Snake's Head ⎫ Fritillary ⎭	*Fritillaria meleagris*	Purple or white	12-18	iv, v	
*Wild Tulip	*Tulipa sylvestris*	Yellow	1-2 ft.	iv, v	
(No English name)	*Lloydia serotina*	White or yellow	6-10	vi	
Yellow Star-of-Bethlehem	*Gagea lutea*	Yellow	6 in.	iii-v	
Star - of - Bethlehem	*Ornithogalum umbellatum*	White	6-9 in.	v, vi	
Spiked Star-of-Bethlehem ⎫ French Sparrowgrass ⎭	*Ornithogalum pyrenaicum*	Yellowish white	1½-2 ft.	vi	
Spring Squill	*Scilla verna*	Grey blue	4-8 in.	v	
Wood Hyacinth ⎫ Culverkeys Bluebell (Eng.) Crawtaes (Scot.) ⎭	*Scilla nutans*	Blue	9-18 in.	iv-v	Many fine garden varieties, white, rose, and red.
Starch Hyacinth	*Muscari racemosum*	Dark blue	6-10 in.	v	
Bog Asphodel	*Narthecium ossifraga*	Golden yellow	6-8 in.	vii, viii	Moist peat.
Saffron Naked Ladies	*Colchicum autumnale*	Rosy mauve	6 in.	ix, x	Many varieties, single and double, white and coloured.

GLASGOW: PRINTED AT THE UNIVERSITY PRESS BY ROBERT MACLEHOSE AND CO. LTD.